The Curse of the *Somers*

The Secret History behind the U.S. Navy's Most Infamous Mutiny

James P. Delgado

OXFORD
UNIVERSITY PRESS

OXFORD
UNIVERSITY PRESS

Oxford University Press is a department of the University of Oxford. It furthers
the University's objective of excellence in research, scholarship, and education
by publishing worldwide. Oxford is a registered trade mark of Oxford University
Press in the UK and certain other countries.

Published in the United States of America by Oxford University Press
198 Madison Avenue, New York, NY 10016, United States of America.

Library of Congress Control Number: 2022943851

ISBN 978–0–19–757522–2

DOI: 10.1093/oso/9780197575222.001.0001

1 3 5 7 9 8 6 4 2

Printed by Sheridan Books, Inc., United States of America

To George and Joel Belcher

What's past is prologue, what to come, in yours and my discharge.

Shakespeare, *The Tempest*, Act 2, Scene 1

CONTENTS

LIST OF ILLUSTRATIONS

PREFACE

The name of the U.S. Brig *Somers* is well known to naval officers more than a century and a half since it became the most infamous ship in the U.S. Navy. The setting for the only "mutiny" on an American warship at sea, *Somers* and its fateful cruise in 1842, which ended in a shipboard "drumhead" trial and the hanging of three men, one of them "but a boy," was a national scandal. It led to a suicide, ruined a career, and brought major changes in how the navy trained its young officers. For decades, the "*Somers* Affair" was a topic not discussed openly by the officers of the U.S. Navy. It was and it remains a highly controversial subject.

The basic facts of the case revolved around the actions of Passed Midshipman Philip Spencer, a nineteen-year-old junior officer, and his actions on board *Somers* while on a voyage to deliver dispatches to the navy's African Squadron, when it was on patrol off the continent's west coast to intercept vessels engaged in the illegal slave trade. *Somers* was no ordinary warship. Although armed, it was a training ship. The two most common American sailing craft of the early nineteenth century were schooners and brigs. *Somers* was a brig: a small, two-masted vessel that carried its sails square-rigged with yards that crossed its masts and a single gaff sail rigged aft, behind the main mast. On the return voyage, Spencer allegedly conspired and led a plot to seize the ship, murder the captain and officers, and take the brig on a piratical cruise. When Captain Alexander Slidell Mackenzie learned of the alleged plot, he had Spencer arrested. A search of Spencer's belongings recovered a paper with names of the crew that suggested a number of co-conspirators to Mackenzie. There was no place to confine Spencer, so he was chained next to one of the brig's guns on the aft deck where the officer at watch by the helm could keep an eye on him.

Over the next few days, Mackenzie and his officers, convinced of a conspiracy, arrested Boatswain's Mate Samuel Cromwell and seaman Elisha Small. Suspicious of the actions of others on the crew, Mackenzie conducted a hearing, but not a proper court-martial, and had his officers interview crew members before returning to Mackenzie with a verdict: death by hanging for Spencer, Cromwell, and Small. *Somers* was two weeks out from New York, where it was homeported at the Brooklyn Navy Yard, but only four days out from St. Thomas in the Virgin Islands. Mackenzie decided to carry out the executions immediately.

On December 1, 1842, Mackenzie assembled the crew, and after a brief speech, allowed Spencer to give the order to fire the gun that was to be the signal to the crew to haul on the lines strung from the end of a yardarm to hang the three men. Spencer could not bring himself to do it, so Mackenzie gave the order. With the roar of the gun, the two men and the boy were hastily hauled up, straining at the ropes that bound them. The men at the lines lowered the bodies, and after preparing their shipmates for burial, committed Spencer, Cromwell, and Small to the deep. For the remainder of the cruise, the officers stood watch with loaded pistols, not catching much sleep, until *Somers* reached Brooklyn with fourteen of the crew restrained and under arrest.

Initial newspaper reports praised Mackenzie and his officers for their bravery, for acting decisively, and for preserving the honor of the navy. Questions soon arose, however. Philip Spencer was no ordinary boy; he was the scapegrace son of John Canfield Spencer, the secretary of war in the administration of President John Tyler. The behavior of the boy notwithstanding, the secretary set out to avenge his son's death at the hands of Captain Mackenzie, insisting on justice. The widow of Samuel Cromwell and the families of some of the accused co-conspirators who had not been hanged joined in public condemnation. Other voices or criticism were added. Mackenzie, an in-law of the prominent, powerful family of Commodore Matthew Calbraith Perry, had made an enemy of author James Fenimore Cooper.

Cooper and Mackenzie had bitterly feuded over Cooper's account of the actions of Oliver Hazard Perry (Matthew's elder brother) and Jesse Duncan Elliott in the Battle of Lake Erie in the War of 1812. Perry, in overall command in the battle, had criticized Elliott's actions, feeling that Elliott, as his second-in-command, had held back his own ship from the main fight while Perry's ship had been mauled in close action with the British. To win the battle, Perry had left his badly damaged ship, *Lawrence*; rowed to Elliott's ship, *Niagara*; and assumed command, emerging victorious. Public praise for both men and the thanks of Congress notwithstanding, the actions of the day and words exchanged between Perry and the proud, spirited Elliott sparked the feud. The bitterness between the two continued until Perry's death on duty in 1819. It remained with Perry's friends and family, however. When Cooper published his *Naval History* in 1839 and shared the laurels of victory with Elliott, Mackenzie's written attack led to his feud with Cooper. Cooper now used the events on *Somers* to attack Mackenzie.

Now known as the "*Somers* Affair," the events of December 1 dominated national news. The court of inquiry and the court-martial were avidly followed, verbatim accounts of the proceedings were published, and it would later be said that nothing more occupied the attention of Americans until the outbreak of the Civil War. The court-martial ultimately acquitted Mackenzie, but his handling of the "mutiny," as it was now seen by some, had stained his reputation. That reputation was not helped when, three days after the verdict, *Somers'* surgeon, Richard Leecock, put a pistol to his head and pulled the trigger in the brig's wardroom. Mackenzie would have to wait years to command another naval vessel, albeit briefly, but thanks to his brother-in-law, Commodore Perry, did serve with distinction in the Mexican War of 1846–1848.

As for *Somers*, its use as a naval training vessel was over. It was assigned to regular sea duties as part of the navy's Home Squadron, cruising the Atlantic Seaboard and the West Indies. It became a point of honor among naval officers to not openly speak of the affair. In 1845, Secretary of the Navy George Bancroft established the U.S. Naval Academy at Annapolis as a direct result of the *Somers* Affair. But while officers did not speak of it, sailors on board the now infamous brig did.

With the outbreak of war with Mexico in 1846, the navy assigned *Somers* to blockade duty off the Gulf port of Veracruz. Its commander was Raphael Semmes, already a legendary naval officer who would gain greater fame and notoriety in the Confederate Navy during the Civil War. *Somers* was patrolling off the port when a ship was spotted that looked as if it might be trying for the port in defiance of the blockade. As *Somers* closed, a squall hit, capsizing the brig as it was "flying light" with few provisions and a full head of sail. Lying on its side, *Somers* quickly filled with water, and in minutes was gone, dragging some of the crew with it and leaving others struggling in the water. Nearby ships saved some, but thirty-six of *Somers'* eighty-man crew were lost.

In the decades that followed, the name of *Somers* was invoked, but by the end of the nineteenth century, the brig had faded from the national consciousness, known only to naval scholars and to the fraternity brothers of Chi Psi. The fraternity, founded by Philip Spencer at Union College in Schenectady, New York, kept his memory alive. To this day, the Chi Psi toast honors Spencer as an unfairly hanged brother, noting that "humanity suffered a blow when Philip Spencer died." In the twentieth century, the name of *Somers* resurfaced nationally with the discovery of a lost manuscript, kept in a chest, unfinished and forgotten following the death of its author, Herman

Melville. Melville's cousin, Guert Gansevoort, was one of the officers on *Somers*. Reportedly plagued by his own role in the controversial events, Gansevoort had turned to drinking, and ultimately ended his naval career "as a sad wreck of his former self, always moody, taciturn and restless."

Gansevoort's tale inspired Melville to make mention of it in his book *White-Jacket* (1850), where he condemned naval discipline, especially flogging, and returned to the subject in his last works; the first was his poem "Billy in the Darbies," published in an 1888 volume of poetry, *John Marr and Other Sailors*, which portrays an innocent youth awaiting death by hanging in "Lone Bay," the ship's jail, his wrists secured by handcuffs, or "darbies." Poignant and powerful, it concludes with the boy lying dead on the seafloor, his execution complete.

Melville began a larger narrative to explain the poem, and was working on it up until a few months before he died in September 1891. Rediscovered in 1921 and finally published in 1924, the novella *Billy Budd, Sailor* resurrected the literary reputation of Herman Melville. Following the success of his earlier books based on his own South Seas adventures as a seaman, *Typee* and *Omoo*, Melville's reputation had waned. *Moby-Dick*, while considered a classic now, and Melville's best work, was roundly criticized and did not sell well. The posthumous publication of *Billy Budd* propelled the man, and his neglected classic, *Moby-Dick*, back into the American, and then the global, literary consciousness.

The story of *Somers* and the resultant "*Somers* Affair" is a very human tale; Melville understood that, as did a number of other writers, including naval scholars, social historians, and those seeking to learn more about a tale that inspired *Billy Budd*. It is that human tale that inspired me. As a maritime archaeologist whose career has largely focused both on lost warships and the nineteenth century, I find *Somers* an obviously compelling tale. It is far more than that, for I am one of the few who has had the privilege of being on *Somers*, experiencing the ship as a wreck.

That experience began with a chance encounter with a friend and fellow maritime archaeologist at the annual meeting of historical and underwater archaeologists, and his sharing the story of how he had been invited to help find a path forward for the protection and study of *Somers*; he was sure that the people who had discovered it, two brothers from Texas, George and Joel Belcher, had indeed found the wreck, and had done so with true and honest intentions to honor *Somers* and all that the wreck represented. They had been turned down by other archaeologists, but they needed to talk to someone who knew ships of the period and had the right connections in the U.S. government. I was the lucky one.

Thus began what is now, more than three decades later, an ongoing saga that drew me in and forged a lifelong friendship. My professional work with George Belcher included other projects around the world, starting with *Somers*, and continuing with other sites and projects such as a series of adventures and work in Vietnam and our final project in the Falkland Islands. We were going to write a book about *Somers* together, but George had been fighting an aggressive cancer that he knew in his heart had come from being sprayed with Agent Orange as he chased Viet Cong during the war. George started a manuscript, but as he grew progressively sick, he laid it aside. I have that manuscript, and it is rightly another tale about George, his adventures, and what wrecks like *Somers* meant to him; powerful stories, and places to preserve. Ever generous in spirit, George went on a buying spree, and for weeks I received copies of every book ever written about *Somers*, the navy at that time, and biographies of the various actors that were associated with the brig *Somers*.

And then he was gone, with his wife Nyugen Thi Lan Huong at his side as he passed in a hospital bed on a gray San Francisco day. Lan Huong and their daughter Lily survive George, but so too does his story. This is not the book George would have written, but it is the book I had to write with a foundation in what George began; the story of *Somers* is timeless and timely, and in reading it, as a human story, I hope that readers in this century will see how much the mid-nineteenth century in America was like our own times; in the scale of time, the 180 years since *Somers'* fatal cruise was "just around the corner," and we in this time live in the reflection of and in consequence of those times. The past is prologue.

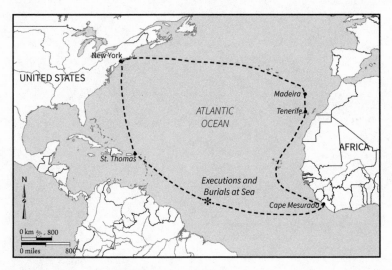

The Ill-Fated Voyage of the U.S. Brig *Somers*, 1842

ACKNOWLEDGMENTS

To my wife, Ann, to whom I usually dedicate my books in addition to the children and our granddaughter, I always owe the biggest debt of gratitude for the time I spend away in my office writing, especially on nights and weekends. Yes, she is a librarian, an avid reader, and an advocate of lifelong learning, but with a still active career, the time I have left to steal to write is often given up by her. To the late George and Joel Belcher, and to Lan Huong and Lily Belcher, who carry George's legacy forward, this hopefully shares more of why George was so special to so many of us. To my editor, Stefan Vranka, Jeremy Toynbee, Zara Cannon-Mohammed, and Timothy DeWerff, all part of the exceptional team at Oxford University Press, my thanks to you for again publishing naval history and archaeology. I also acknowledge the review and edits made by Dr. William Dudley, Dr. Craig Symonds, and Dr. Michael Brennan, who made many helpful suggestions on the manuscript for this book as friends and colleagues.

The *Somers* saga was introduced to me first by Mitch Marken, fellow archaeologist. He graciously introduced me to George and Joel Belcher, and I made my first dive on *Somers* with Mitch. We've been friends ever since. I also want to thank Santiago Analco, Edward "Ned" Beach, Edwin C. Bearss, Peter Bernhardt, Rowland Bowers, John Brooks, Mary Sue Conaway, David L. Conlin, Michael

Crawford, Monica Cuevas y Lara, William S. Dudley, Pilar Luna Erreguerena, Kevin J. Foster, Joaquin Garcia-Bárcena, Elizabeth Gardner, Robert Gelbard, Santos Gómez Leyva, the late Senator Howell Heflin (D-AL), Roberto Junco, Harold D. Langley, Daniel J. Lenihan, Jerry Livingston, Philip McFarland, Larry E. Murphy, Juan Enrique Suárez Peredo Navarette, Larry V. Nordby, Andrew Oltyan, Eugene Pinkelmann, Juan Rique, J. Ashley Roach, Jerry L. Rogers, Matthew Russell, William N. Still, and Alberto Vazquez de la Cerda.

I also acknowledge the support, assistance, and access to archives and records by the Armada de México, Tercer Distrito Naval; the crew of *Margarita Maza de Juárez*, Veracruz, México; Commandos Subacuaticos of the Armada de México, Acapulco; the National Park Service's Submerged Resources Center, Denver, Colorado; U.S. Department of State, Washington, DC; the office of the late Senator Howell Heflin; U.S. Naval Institute, Annapolis; National Archives, Washington, DC, and College Park, Maryland; Naval History and Heritage Command, Washington, DC; Instituto Nacional de Antropología e Historia, Mexico City; Library of Congress, Washington, DC; Museo Nacional de las Intervenciones, Mexico City; U.S. Naval Academy Museum, Annapolis; and New-York Historical Society, New York. Any errors and omissions found are my responsibility.

Introduction

The First of December 1842

We make our address to thy divine Majesty; in this our necessity, that thou wouldest take the cause into thine own hand, and judge between us and our enemies.

— *The Book of Common Prayer, 1842*

It was a day like any other of the preceding week. It began simply as the sun rose, climbing into the sky to reveal a vast, empty sea. A small vessel, rigged as a two-masted brig, is alone on the sea. Large swells of dark water roll past the ship, lifting it as the hull languorously slices through them, leaving a wake of froth and swirling eddies of water. The breeze is moderate, and the thick canvas of the sails is full but not straining as the wind drives the ship steadily and slowly ahead. It is a peaceful scene, a calm day at sea. But it is not calm on the ship.

Three men, their wrists and ankles bound, stand on the deck, surrounded by the rest of the crew, most of them boys or young men. Interspersed around the deck are the ship's officers and petty officers, armed with pistols and cutlasses, intently watching the massed crew as they stand in silent ranks. Three lines of rope, known to these men not as *rope* but as *lines* and in this use as *whips*, all part of the specialized language of seamen, are looped through wooden blocks at the ends of the yards, or as the sailors know them, from the *yardarms*. The whips dangle from the yardarms straight down to the deck. At the end of each whip is one of the three men, head covered by cloth and a noose around their neck. Not yet dead, but already shrouded.

Groups of sailors stand ready at each line, on either side of the foremast. Death is soon to step aboard and tension and fear are barely controlled. The crew watch the three figures, soon to be shipmates no more. For many of the crew—most of them boys, some as young as thirteen—this will be their first encounter with violent death.

The three men are silent. One of them struggles to say something, but he chokes. He cannot utter the words he must say. He asks another officer to step forward and says, "I cannot do it. Please ask the captain to give the word." The other officer turns to the captain, and says, "Mr. Spencer asks that you give the word, sir." The captain does not hesitate, and shouts, "Stand by!" and then "Fire!" A hot coal touches the wick of a nearby cannon, and the roar of the blast comes as fire shoots out of the muzzle, and a thundering boom echoes across the water. Another officer shouts, "Whip!" The crew grab each line and run, steadily pulling the three men up to the yard-arms, leaving them hanging more than thirty feet off the deck. At the same time, the ship's flag and its pennant also whip up, the thirteen stripes and twenty-six stars showing that this is an American vessel, and the pennant showing that this is a vessel of the U.S. Navy. It is 2:15 in the afternoon, a half hour after all hands had been called on deck to bear witness.

This hanging carries none of the neck-snapping jolt of falling through a gallows. This is slow death by strangulation. The nooses tighten and squeeze shut the carotid arteries, cutting off the flow of blood to the brain. The pain is excruciating. In the first seconds, they lose control of their bowels, staining their britches. Their tracheas, nearly crushed by the unrelenting pressure, stop delivering oxygen to their lungs. They struggle to get their arms free before going into violent convulsions that last for several minutes. The convulsions continue even when they are unconscious. This is a gruesome death. Sometime between twenty to forty minutes after the three men are pulled into the air by their shipmates, they are finally dead, motionless but swaying at the end of each whip with the movement of the ship. Beneath the hoods that shroud their faces, their eyes bulge, their faces turn purple and then black. The whips, taut with the weight of each body, are secured to the pin rails, wrapped a few times around a belaying pin. There is no need for the crew to stand and hold their dead shipmates aloft long enough to ensure that they are dead, but the next hour will make sure that they are.

They hang as below them the crew muster aft, near the stern around the captain, as he stands, resplendent in his uniform and atop an elevated area on the aft deck that provides more headroom for the officers' and crews' mess. From this makeshift pulpit, the captain lectures his shocked, frightened crew of boys and men. The men whom they have just helped kill, he explained, had failed moral tests, succumbed to greed and "brutish sensuality," and met a fate that they could not avoid if they did not adhere to living and serving with truth, honor, and fidelity. He says those three words with strict emphasis.

The sermon done, he turns to the boatswain's mate, and gives the order, "Pipe down from witnessing punishment!" Raising his brass whistle to his lips, the boatswain issues two short, shrill blasts followed by a warbling call. The crew relaxes. Their shoulders stoop, arms hang freely, and some softly exhale. The captain shouts, "Stand by, to give three hearty cheers for the flag of our country!" He starts the refrain. "Hip, Hip" and the crew respond with a loud "Huzzah!" "Hip, Hip, Huzzah!" and for the last time, even louder, "Hip, Hip, Huzzah!" The captain gives a tight, slight smile. All eyes turn from the flag fluttering from the masthead, and the captain turns to the boatswain again and shouts, "Pipe down, and Pipe to Dinner!"

The whistle sounds. The crew break into smaller groups, joining their messmates, who are the seamen with whom they are assigned to berth and eat. As this day has shown, naval life is regulated. It is disciplined. And yet some of the boys look up and call out to the three unmoving figures, laughing and insulting the corpses. Other boys, some with tears in their eyes, are silent. They go below for an hour, out of sight of the three dead men who dangle from the yardarms as the ship continues to sail toward the sinking sun. The three men have been hanging for fifteen minutes; it is now 2:30 in the afternoon.

The hour passes, and at 3:30 the captain gives the order to lower the bodies. A line of sailors again grabs each whip and supports the weight as the line is taken off the belaying pin that has held it, and then, hand over hand, the crew slowly lowers each body to the deck, limp though already stiffening. They are laid out on the deck, and the nooses are cut free. Each man is surrounded by his former messmates, who have the task to prepare them for burial. The hoods are removed, revealing each man's swollen, blood-dark face in its final grimace. The bodies are stripped, washed, and dressed in clean clothes brought up from their sea chests or sea bags. Their hair is trimmed. These final intimacies reveal the wear and injury of a life at sea, but on the body of the older, large seaman, a series of scars on his head, the mark of cutlass blows, stand out. This was a man who knew violence.

Darkness is coming, and the captain and his first lieutenant inspect the bodies as their messmates stand by. Spencer is dressed in his full dress uniform, as befits his rank of midshipman. But his sword belt is empty, as the verdict has taken away that right. His hands are bound, not to confine, but to keep the corpse's arms in position. The other two bodies are also dressed, and the captain looks down to see that the large, scarred sailor's hands are bound not with twine, but with the black silk ribbon that once graced his sailor's hat. This "tally band" spells out the ship's name in gold letters: SOMERS. The captain frowns and pauses, and then moves on to the last body. As he does, a flash of lightning, a gust, and a heavy rain hit the ship. The superstitious men look down and mutter a prayer, while other hands, seasoned and content with the knowledge that sudden squalls strike at sea, carry on as the captain gives the order to drape canvas tarps over the bodies.

The squall ends after the sun disappears over the horizon. The ship sails on in the dark. With no other light to interfere, the universe above is on full, brightly colored display. On a dark, reflective sea, the boundaries between sky and sea blur; it is almost as if the ship is now drifting through space itself, alone in this vastness. The illusion retreats as lanterns are lit and hung around the deck, giving off an orange glow that illuminates the scene. Spencer's body is lifted and placed in a large wooden coffin fashioned from two mess chests emptied of their stores to give the disgraced officer a formal burial as befits his rank. Holes bored in the bottom will quickly flood the coffin when it is dropped into the sea. It is too big for the body, but solid iron cannonballs—known to these seamen as *shot*—are laid inside the coffin to weight it to sink.

The messmates of the other two men lay their bodies in their hammocks; they will sleep for eternity in these thick canvas shrouds. The hammocks are large enough to enclose the bodies; in a crowded berth deck in a sailing ship, a hammock offers a rare opportunity for privacy, even when swinging with the swell directly next to other hammocks and their occupants. As the canvas is drawn over the bodies, also weighted with shot, the sailmaker kneels and, with his heavy needle and twine, stitches the hammock shut. There is a sailors' superstition that the dead will return from the sea and haunt the ship unless the last stitch goes through the dead man's nose. Seamen are a superstitious lot. The older men, with years of service at sea, fervently want to see the heavy, triangular point of the needle make that stitch.

The three bodies are laid out, lying in pools of light in a row, Spencer farthest aft. The captain orders the flag lowered to half-mast. The crew cluster around the crowded deck, prayer books in hand, as the captain removes his hat and opens his Book of Common Prayer. Reading from the page that begins the Order for the Burial of the Dead, the captain starts with the Gospel of St. John: "I am the resurrection and the life." As he reads, the crew follows, and give the responses, as the captain will later recall, "both audibly and devoutly." As he reads the lines to commit the bodies to the deep, sailors tilt the three planks that the coffin and shrouds rest upon, and they slide into the sea, disappearing into the darkness. As they sink, fathoms down into the deep, the Lord's Prayer follows.

The captain pauses and reads the prayer in the book "to be used at sea" for morning and evening services. With what has transpired on this day, he gives particular emphasis to "Preserve us from the dangers of the sea, and from the violence of the enemy," so that "we may be a safeguard unto the United States of America, and a security for such as pass on the sea in their lawful occasions," before closing and the crew's response, ending, "by thy mercy, obtain everlasting life, through Jesus Christ our Lord. Amen."

At the captain's order, the boatswain pipes down and dismisses the officers and crew, who turn to their own beds and hammocks. The day ends as *Somers* sails on, bound for home. Discipline has been maintained, a terrible price has been paid by the three dead, and others in the crew sleep confined and manacled, awaiting trial ashore, but not executed on this day. No one is under any illusion; this matter is far from over, and *Somers* and its officers and crew are sailing into a figurative storm unlike any seen by them or their country.

Chapter 1

Philip Spencer

There was trouble brewing from the moment Philip Spencer stepped on board the brig *Somers*. Spencer was both *trouble* and *troubled*, as he would quickly find himself on this small, highly regimented naval training vessel. The nineteen-year-old scapegrace son of a prominent man found himself immediately at odds with his captain and the other officers. Some of it was due to his well-deserved bad reputation. Joining the crew of the small ship run by an autocratic captain, Spencer was alone and not liked.

As on all ships, space was at a premium, and every available compartment, locker, or place to hang a bag was put to use, even if only for storage. *Somers* was only a hundred feet long, twenty-five feet wide at its maximum extent, and the hold, in which the compartments were fitted, was eleven feet high. It was packed tight with provisions, powder, and shot for the ten cannon, with very few opportunities for privacy in a vessel carrying 107 crew and thirteen officers. A seaman might say that there was not enough room to swing a cat; the phrase is from the days of wooden ships and harshly run navies and it refers to a tight space where the "cat," or the cat-o'-nine-tails, a braided whip used to discipline and punish sailors, would be swung with force, again and again, into the bare back of a sailor. As events on *Somers* would soon show, while too crowded below deck, there was plenty of room to swing a cat on the deck.

The wardroom, a ten-by-six-foot space below deck at the stern, was the exclusive territory of the officers. But for a junior officer, and especially for Philip Spencer, it was not always a welcome space. For the right midshipman (the lowest officer's rank in the navy at that time), it could be. But the wardroom was on this voyage occupied by a tight-knit family that exclusively shunned Spencer. Just forward of the wardroom, the "steerage" was the territory where Spencer shared meals and a sleeping space with six other midshipmen, the brig's junior officers. Four feet long and fourteen feet wide, nearly half of the steerage was taken up by the brig's pumps and a table. Seven canvas hammocks, lashed and stowed by day, were hung at night from the deck beams; Philip Spencer's was slung "over the door leading from the berth deck," where the crew slept "through the steerage to the ward-room."[1] Anyone passing by his hammock at night would brush against it. The rest of the crew slept in the berth deck, a fifty-by-seventeen-foot compartment that stretched between the brig's two masts, slinging their hammocks.

Into this overcrowded world, yet isolated at sea, Spencer would in the course of this voyage be arrested, confined, quickly tried, and then along with two others, hanged at sea on charges of inciting mutiny. The incident did not quickly pass into history as just another episode in the long history of seafaring, sea fights, and mutinies. It became a national scandal, inspired—and still inspiring—spirited debate, with questions about what really happened, and if the executions were both justified *and* legal. Spencer, either victim or villain, neither, or a little of both, has occupied center stage since the news broke in December 1842. For a young man who died just shy of his twentieth birthday, Spencer is one of the most notorious figures in the history of the U.S. Navy. Very little, other than notes made as he rambled his defense and pled for his life, survives to speak for him, while much has been written about him. Into that gap have stepped shipmates, classmates, family friends, his father, his accusers, and a century and a half's analysis by journalists and historians. What emerges is that the major problem, the crux of the tragedy to come, was that Spencer's troubled personality—born of physical disability, a confused childhood, and something in "the blood," a family inheritance of behavior—collided with his new captain's own insecurities.

They were oil and water. His captain would lose his reputation; Spencer would lose his life.

That life began on January 28, 1823, in Canandaigua, New York, a small town on the shores of one of the Finger Lakes below Lake Ontario. Canandaigua, which in Seneca means "the chosen spot," was the setting for a smal planned community founded not long after the American Revolution. The founder, Oliver Phelps, had grand designs, hoping to make this new village "a place full of people; residents, surveyors, explorers, adventurers . . . a busy, thriving place."[2] Spencer was born in a "brown painted house, setting a little back from the street, not large, but cozy." The home, then three decades old, had been purchased in 1809 by Philip's father.

Opposite the home, in a large open field, stood the Canandaigua Academy, where Philip would later attend school. Canandaigua then was a small village with around two thousand inhabitants and approximately 350 buildings. With the construction of the Erie Canal, the village grew into a town, though to this day, two and a half centuries after its founding, Canandaigua still remains a quaint town of some ten thousand people.[3] That small community of two hundred years ago, then just a few hundred, was where the Spencers settled, a family with roots that reached back to late eighteenth-century Connecticut. A family historian, introducing an "individual memorial of an honest lineage" in 1902, noted that "our link is part of a great chain."[4] That "chain" represented continuity with all of its requisite legacies and burdens. An early twentieth-century account of Canandaigua qualified Philip Spencer's fate by stating that he had been "High born and high bred."[5] The first family home in Canandaigua was a "severely plain but commodious frame house" built by Philip's grandfather, Ambrose Spencer.

Ambrose launched himself professionally and personally while studying with lawyer John Canfield and boarding in his home at age eighteen. He also secretly courted Canfield's fourteen-year-old daughter, Laura. The two married, clandestinely, and ostensibly remained chaste for several months before telling his mentor, now father-in-law, the news. The family histories recorded no split, perhaps because Papa Canfield realized that Ambrose needed marriage "to mould and fashion his strong will, peculiar temperament and forceful mind into channels of ambition, courage and steadiness."[6] Ambrose Spencer had a long life and a distinguished legal and political career, serving as attorney general for New York, then as a justice, and finally as chief justice in the New York Supreme Court. When he retired he was elected mayor of Albany and then a state legislator.

Judge Spencer was well connected, and it was said that he was "one of the dictators of New York State at the time when politics knew no law."[7] Politics, as twentieth-century British politician Aneurin "Nye" Bevan would state, "is a blood sport," and Ambrose Spencer took that precept to heart.[8] When Laura Canfield Spencer died, Ambrose married the daughter of New York governor DeWitt Clinton, one of his closest allies. That did not stop him from feuding with Clinton, and even his wife was "unable to prevent Spencer from quarrelling with her father and driving him out of politics."[9] When the second Mrs. Spencer died, he married her sister. Respected, feared, and probably as "severely plain" as his Canandaigua house, but with a quietly rebellious streak, Ambrose Spencer was likely a son of a bitch.

Ambrose and Laura Spencer's first child, born in January 1788, was John Canfield Spencer, Philip's father. Like his father, John Canfield Spencer was an attorney, a one-term congressman, member of the New York State Assembly, then a senator, and finally a Cabinet secretary, both for War and the Treasury. The acorn had not fallen far from the tree in regard to personality, it seems. "He never was an attractive man, because his ambition was kiln-dried."[10] Nathan Sargent, a nineteenth-century political historian, more charitably described Spencer as "a man of great abilities, industry, and endurance, curt manners and irascible temper." A family friend joined the ranks of half-complimentary appraisals, noting that John Canfield Spencer was "stern, uncompromising, obstinate in temper, determined and energetic in action."[11] That less than complimentary local reminiscence, safely published a half century after his death, observed that John Canfield Spencer "was undoubtedly a very able lawyer, as his father, in spite of his personal imperfections, had been a great judge."[12] But the writer of the reminiscence also noted, whether spurred by enmity, or relaying gossip, that "the law in this family served to drive out the ordinary sources of affection and pleasure."

FIGURE 1.1 John Canfield Spencer

John Canfield Spencer was also an advocate of American democracy, not aristocracy, nor cabals, a seemingly incongruous aspect of a man whose father was noted as a behind-the-scenes manipulator of politics and power. Perhaps as much as the son followed the father, he also eschewed aspects of his politics. The Freemasons had been a prominent part of the foundation of the new Republic, and a number of prominent Americans, including George Washington, were members; the Eye of Providence, a Masonic symbol, is depicted both on the Great Seal of the United States and the modern one-dollar bill.

The prominence of the Masons and a sense they were controlling the new nation's government, to the detriment of the common man, led to resentment. Anti-Masonic sentiment boiled over after the mysterious disappearance of Canandaigua stonemason William Morgan in 1826. Morgan, arrested for debt, disappeared after his release. The fact that Morgan had just published a tell-all book exposing the secret rituals of the Freemasons led many to believe—although his body was never found—that he had been kidnapped and murdered before he spilled all he knew. This ignited a national fervor, reviving a "dormant hostility to Freemasonry and all secret societies," which in time led to the formation of a new American political party, the Anti-Masons.[13] It was a national scandal. John Canfield Spencer first gained national prominence as a special counsel—much like a modern special counsel seeking evidence of high crimes and misdemeanors.

For five years, trials of defendants arrested for the kidnapping and probable murder of Morgan filled the newspapers. While there was never any resolution, John Canfield Spencer became nationally famous, and soon joined the new Anti-Mason political party, as did his father. The Anti-Masonic Party in short time would be annexed into the newly formed Whig Party. Daniel Webster, political sage that he was, wrote to Ambrose Spencer in November 1831, on the eve of the Anti-Masonic Party Convention, asking him not to attend and tie himself too closely, as the anti-Masons as a political movement would not sustain a national win. "Anti-Masonry as a sentiment, is gaining ground, but Anti-Masonry as a political party, or the basis of such party, I do not think is gaining. Our people do not feel that Anti-Masonry alone, is a principle broad enough to save the Country & maintain the Govt."[14] The Whigs would come to dominate American politics before being subsumed by the newly formed Republican Party as the issue of slavery split the party in 1856.

John Canfield Spencer also gained fame for hosting Alexis de Tocqueville at his home in Canandaigua in 1831, as de Tocqueville made the tour that would result in *Democracy in America*, a book that John Canfield Spencer would then translate into English. The concept of democracy extending the sphere of individual freedom, repudiating aristocracy, and the rise of equality was powerful. John Spencer was de Tocqueville's original American editor and in 1851 Spencer wrote a detailed analysis of his work; among his interesting observations was in regard to the government and navy given the power to compel service through conscription of the British system of "impressment." When enough seamen could not be induced to enlist, roving, armed gangs were paid a bounty by the navy to simply seize men who were then "impressed" into service against their will. But, wrote Spencer, "the difficulty is to induce the people ... to submit to impressment or any compulsory system."[15] This fundamental aspect of naval life would be dramatically challenged by Spencer's own son on *Somers*.

Into this family, and to this father and his wife, the former Elizabeth Scott Smith, Philip arrived as one of seven children, three daughters and four sons, two of whom died young. When Philip was born in 1823, he had two older sisters, Laura and Mary, who were thirteen and eleven years older; a third sister, Eliza, had died as a baby. Philip had two older brothers, Ambrose, who was six years older, and John Jr. Following Philip was the "baby" of the family, his brother DeWitt. But when DeWitt died at age six, when Philip was thirteen, he was suddenly the youngest and the last child at home. One of his teachers at that time recalled that Philip was consequently "petted by his mother and family."[16] His bond with his mother was particularly strong; his father was often absent, leaving Elizabeth Spencer to raise the children.

Influenced by his mother, as her "pet," Philip also had inherited traits from his father, both through nature and nurture. As his life progressed, the boy, like his father and grandfather before him, was hot-tempered, obstinate, and self-focused. As one account would later note, the tendency of the older Spencers was to always be "contriving something—starting some political game," and this would later be seen by some as perhaps the inheritance of Philip Spencer, who died "merely the victim of this school of design—restless, intriguing, plotting to do something large and striking, before he had reached time and experience to get at something legitimate." But there was also something more, a physical "defect" as it would be called in the day, and one that two centuries later still brings a host of psychosocial problems. One of Philip's classmates noted "that he had a decided cast in his eyes and that otherwise he would have been thought good-looking, if not handsome."

The cast to his eyes was strabismus, known cruelly as being "wall-eyed," "squint-eyed," or "cross-eyed" or the inevitable school yard taunt of being a "wall-eyed bastard" or a "wall-eyed son of a bitch." Philip had "inherited it" from his father since the elder Spencer had strabismus. What role strabismus played in his father's life is unknown, but John Canfield Spencer had a lifelong reputation for being angry and contentious. While we do not know exactly what the nature of their strabismus was, this meant that one of their eyes was unable to achieve proper alignment. This could be one eye pointing to his nose, one eye pointing away from the nose, one eye turned downward, or one eye pointed upward. Strabismus can lead to psychological and social problems. One of the first things we notice about each other when we meet are the other person's features, including their eyes. An eye that is askew stands out, and as Philip's classmate averred, this kept Philip from being seen as handsome, or even good-looking. Whether you are the pet of your family at home or not, that leaves scars on the soul.

In 1841, eye surgeon Alfred C. Post wrote that "the most striking effect of strabismus is the deformity which it occasions, frequently subjecting the patient during childhood to ridicule and insult, and being throughout life a source of mortification and mental disquietude."[17] In modern times, what emerges from clinical studies and medical literature is that children with noticeable strabismus are viewed negatively, not only by their peers, but by adults as well. At an early age, anxiety, depression, and responses to this rejection lead to schizophrenia, while vision problems can contribute to poor academic achievement and difficulty in life.

What emerges from various accounts of Philip Spencer's young life is a clear picture of a highly intelligent, emotionally scarred child, with a distant, yet powerful and opinionated father, a family heritage of expectations, and a loving but obsessively close mother. To the outside world, especially fellow children and his classmates, he would show two sides of his nature; friendly, open, sensitive, even loving but also vicious. At an early age, he also adopted a playfulness about his strabismus, in order to gain acceptance by poking fun at his own eyes. This is all part of a Philip who emerged through his teen years as a schizophrenic personality, beguiling to some, repellant to others.

When Philip was eight in 1831, his oldest sister, Mary, left home after her marriage, and the following year, in 1832, his other sister, Laura, was married. His two older brothers, Ambrose and John Jr., were, as events in their lives would attest, as troubled as Philip and their father, but not as disciplined as the old man. Philip's teacher, Samuel Howe, late in life remembered that Philip's problems, like his brothers', were exacerbated by alcohol. The two older boys frequently raided John Canfield Spencer's wine cellar, sending Philip "when they wished to have a drinking carousal with their boon companions . . . to get a bottle from the cellar. And Mrs. Spencer, it is reported, would so change the bottles that Mr. Spencer could not, or would not be likely to detect it." Professor Howe, who was Philip's teacher at that time, said that Philip "contracted a relish for strong drink," abetted by the "indulgence of the mother," who "because the father was strict or severe, would hide the fault."[18]

Indulgences by his mother extended, as the other children left, to Elizabeth Spencer keeping Philip close to home instead of sending him off to school. The Canandaigua Academy, established in 1791 as a private boys' school and standing in an open, tree-dotted square next to the Spencer home, had matured as an institution and recently undergone an expansion and modification. A three-story, imposing brick building, it was the equivalent of a modern high school, and since 1828 had been directed by Professor Howe, who was the principal as well as a teacher. Under Howe, the academy became financially self-sufficient and then expanded, and this was the "new" school that Philip Spencer attended.

The boy who arrived and began classes at Canandaigua's primary department at age twelve in 1836, recalled Howe, was a "little roguish fellow" who "was the ruling spirit, getting others into sport, and escaping detection himself" but he "was not a favorite of the schoolboys. Once they set upon him with so much violence, that Mrs. Spencer kept him out of school several days, and wrote . . . that his teacher should interpose with his schoolmates, and cause them to desist from their talks and taunts, as Philip was not at fault." Professor Howe, late in life, reproduced the note from Elizabeth Spencer in a reminiscence of his own career:

> It will give me pleasure, Mr. Howe, to have you call over to-morrow, or any time that you have leisure. I want to talk over that "little matter" about Philip. As he is so very sensitive on the subject, I told him I would see you myself before he went to school again. He had a severe attack the night before, so that we sent for the doctor, and he is hardly well enough to be out to-day. With respect, E. S. S

The little matter may have been his strabismus. Additionally, Howe remembered that Philip also "found that he could cross his eyes, in sport; partly by this practice, and partly by inheritance, (for his father's eyes were so), they got set in a sort of a twist, or twinkle, of his sight."

Making fun of his own "odd cast" did not win many friends. A classmate from that time, after Philip's death, remembered him as "a sprightly, delicate lad who was quite a favorite with many of his schoolmates, though his queer stories and sharp tricks made him quite unpopular with others."[19] He'd be quick to anger at what he perceived to be injustice, or restrictions, and when he got in trouble, his parents would be there ready to bail him out. Five decades later, Howe remembered him sadly but fondly, noting the injustice of his death and that "Philip was shrewd enough, while under the writer's care in school, for two years, to escape any serious correction. They were the twelfth and thirteenth years of his short life."[20]

Graduating from the Canandaigua Academy, Philip left home at fourteen to attend Geneva College, in the same county as Canandaigua, Ontario County. Geneva, another private academy, established in 1807, had struggled financially, closed and reopened with the financial support and under the leadership of the Episcopal Diocese of New York in 1822, becoming a college in 1825. Now boarding at the school, and not living at home, Philip began to falter. One of his teachers recalled that "he was overbearing, intolerant, cruel, fond of reading impractical books and also intemperate in his habits." His favorite book, published the year before, was *The Pirates Own Book; or, Authentic Narratives of the Lives, Exploits, and Executions of the Most Celebrated Sea Robbers*, complete with a lurid engraving on the title page showing a pirate "carrying the Dutch girl on board."

The Pirates Own Book had a singular impact on Philip; this was one of, if not the leading, "impractical books" his teacher at Geneva criticized him for reading. The book had to be compelling to the boy who had found himself shunned by some for his eye, and with few friends he trusted, and then perhaps doubting that they really liked him, but were there because of his family's standing, or because he would amuse them by playing the clown by mocking his own deformity. There is an aspect of behavior that suggests that if one cannot command love, then they can command fear, or through fear, respect. The preface, therefore, had meaning as "there is a superstitious horror connected with the name of Pirate; there are few subjects that interest and excite the curiosity of mankind generally, more than the desperate exploits, foul doings, and diabolical nature of these monsters in human form." And yet the pirate could escape capture and punishment by selecting "the most lonely isles of the sea for his retreat," or when "he secretes himself near the shores of rivers, bays and lagoons of thickly wooded and uninhabited countries, so that if pursued he can escape to the woods and mountain glens of the interior."[21] Professor Howe, late in life, remembered that "Philip, when a boy, was noted for a brilliant imagination. This was excited still more by reading again and again the 'The Pirate's Own Book.' That book destroyed him."[22]

At Geneva, classmate Paul F. D. Cooper remembered that "his manner was remarkably good, quiet, courteous, and self-possessed. His voice was very low and pleasant. . . . He seemed to live by himself and to mingle little with other students. If he had any intimates I do not know who they were, and my belief is that there were none. His class standing for scholarship and attendance was very low. . . . In one thing he excelled the whole college. He was by far the best declaimer I have ever heard with the exception of one or two men whose reputation is national." Spencer's manner, he recalled, was "more like that of a high-bred man of the world than a boy's just growing into manhood."[23]

Classmate I. H. McCollum later recalled in his own reminiscence of Philip Spencer that their class of 1842 had dwindled from about twenty freshmen to seven seniors at commencement. Spencer "was one of those who dropped out by the way. He was a talented young man, very quick to learn, pleasant and companionable, and to those whose kindness justified it, confiding. He seldom mingled with the students in their sports and games on the campus." In addition, "The ease with which he mastered the Greek and Latin was remarkable" and

FIGURE 1.2 Philip Spencer

Spencer assisted older students so much his own studies were hurt. "I do not remember Spencer as vicious or reckless or a mischief-making young man. Whilst his habits were inclined to indolence he had a great self-will and firmness when occasion called it out. . . . He had an ear for music and played fairly well on violin and cornopaean [cornet].[24]"

Spencer's grasp of Greek and Latin came from his earlier studies at Canandaigua, where Professor Howe recalled that he learned not only by reading but by speaking them, and thus for him, they were living languages, but perhaps there was also a sense of being able to hold something to himself, to keep it secret and safe. At the academy, Philip had proudly made a catalog, or list, of his teachers and fellow students in these dead languages. Now, at Geneva, he ignored most of his studies except ancient languages, and while seen as a linguist, he was accused of being academically lazy. Philip's surviving academic record suggests that he had not so shrewdly avoided correction at Geneva as he did at Canandaigua. On February 21, 1840, for example, he was listed as being negligent and "going to Canandaigua without permission," and was sent to Greene, a small community nearly a hundred miles southeast of Geneva, "to remain for a time under the care of Rev. I. V. Van Iryen." Another disciplinary incident, recorded on November 23, 1840, notes that Philip Spencer "was a participant in the cider disturbance, so-called," but does not appear to have been regarded as a leading spirit.[25]

More damning testimony comes from his Canandaigua teacher, Professor Howe, who said that at Geneva, Spencer "committed many lawless deeds for obtaining money. He went into a bookstore and examined a case of surgical instruments and had them laid aside, when he should call again with the cash. But, watching when the clerk was in, he said to him, I will take those instruments which I purchased. He went out and sold them to a student of the Medical Department for what he could get. At another time he went to the room of a religious student and pretended to be very serious. But, he said: "I cannot become a Christian until I pay a debt of five dollars which I owe. 'The pious student was deceived and gave Spencer the money, when with a well-known college call he gathered his comrades, went down town and had a drinking bout.' "[26]

The duality, or perhaps the schizophrenic nature, of Philip Spencer shows through at Geneva in two tales. Remaining a freshman and not academically advancing at one graduation, Spencer joined an academic procession at the end of the parade, wearing a dunce's cap with a streamer that read "Patriarch of the Freshman Class," with college officials at the front oblivious to his game.[27] The other tale, from McCollum's reminiscence, noted that while at Geneva, Spencer underwent an operation to correct his strabismus, "and refused to be bound or held during the operation," which to McCollum was proof of his "self-will and firmness," but also likely reflected a strong desire to correct an obvious aspect that influenced a first impression of Philip Spencer, even before he would speak.[28]

Strabismus surgery, then being introduced, involved tightening or replacing the muscles of the inner eye in an age *without* anesthetic. While nitrous oxide and ether were known, McCollum's memoir suggests Philip, like nearly all patients in the first half of the nineteenth century, had none, which is why they were both "bound" or held down, usually in an operating chair. Any surgery at that time was both brutal and risky.

The surgery, with the help of two or three aides, placed the patient "in a sitting posture, facing a window, with his head leaning against the breast of an assistant, or he may lie upon a table or sofa," sometimes passing "a folded sheet around the body of the patient and the table upon which he lies, so as to prevent him from moving." The surgeon then applied "iced water or snow for a few minutes over the closed eye-lids, for the purpose of contracting the vessels of the conjunctiva, and diminishing the hemorrhage during the operation." With the other eye covered "to enable the patient to direct the affected eye outwards," the surgeon then "fixed" the eye by holding it or using a hook, and then slicing into conjunctiva to reach the muscle.[29]

The surgery failed, but even had it not, it likely would not have changed Philip. In April 1841, an entry in the college's records notes that on that day Philip Spencer, "at the request of his father received a dismission from the college. The request was made in consequence of his continued neglect of college exercises and this neglect stated in the letter of dismission; but inasmuch as a change of association might prove favorable, it was also stated that the faculty of this college would make no objection on account of his deficient standing here, to his immediate reception at any other college."[30] That reception, forthcoming and thanks to his father, was at Union College in Schenectady, where John Canfield Spencer, himself a graduate, had been a regent since 1840. Before leaving Geneva, Philip Spencer gifted his copy of *The Pirates Own Book* to the Geneva College Society. He gave the book away, but he never forgot it.

While the academic side of and the requisite discipline of college life were clearly not what Philip Spencer wanted, one aspect of
Union was very attractive. Known today as the "mother of fraterni-
ties," Union is where the three oldest, still existing Greek societies
in American academia were formed. Kappa Alpha (1825), Sigma
Phi (1827), and Delta Phi (1827), the "Union Triad," were followed by Psi Epsilon in 1833. The very thought of a secret society—
something his anti-Masonic father would bridle at—must have held
some attraction for a rebellious son. There was also a chance to focus
on his love of ancient Greek, as well as a secret society that had an
aspect of the band of brothers he probably imagined pirates to be.
With classmate James Lafayette Witherspoon and others, Philip
Spencer formed Chi Psi, "which was against the rules of the College,
as forsooth there were enough societies already."[31]

A key and important point was that, as Witherspoon later recalled,
Spencer did not want to join any of the existing secret societies, as
"Phil Spencer . . . did not like the kind of men who composed the
other secret societies" and proposed forming "a new society, to be
composed of kindred spirits." Spencer "gave most of his time to the
business of organization, devised the signs, grips and pass words."
Looking back decades later, Witherspoon recalled his fraternal
brother as "a tall man of dark complexion, with black hair and eyes,
and noble-hearted and generous to a fault. He always took great
delight in the initiations, grips, signs and pass words, and studied
how to make them more mysterious and impressive."[32] But to others,
including his professors, Spencer was not a serious scholar, was not
popular beyond his fraternity, and had a reputation for wild stories
and getting into "slight scrapes."[33] Philip's tenure at Union College
was therefore short, as he was soon dismissed and returned home.

An unnamed friend and messmate, in a January 1843 memoir
on Philip Spencer, said that Spencer, "being of a wandering turn of
mind, and fond of any thing bordering on the dangerous and mar-
velous . . . eloped from his home and went to New-York; concealing
his parentage shipped for a whaler fitting out at Nantucket . . . [and]

was sent to the latter place in a small schooner."[34] The friend could not understand what drove Spencer to this—perhaps not having read *The Pirates Own Book* or understanding Spencer's naïve sense of the pull of the sea as a place to be free:

> He smiled at my astonishment at his deserting his happy, luxurious and delightful home; and, now as I look back, as I often have since, I think of that smile of Spencer—yes, as I now write, I can see as distinct as the words I am penning—that smile was not human! The wild rolling of his eyes told plainly enough, to any one at all discerning, that something was working in that heart that could not submit to the dull monotony of this peaceful, every day life. His reply was that he "should like to harpoon a whale and the blood spilt," that he "was not afraid of danger and liked an adventurous life."[35]

At Nantucket, as the whaler was fitting out for what would be a voyage of a year or more's duration, Spencer joined a small vessel to hunt for "black fish" (small whales, usually Pilot whales that yielded little oil) but was caught in the gale of October 1841—a storm that lashed the coast from October 2 to 4 and wrecked nearly two hundred ships. The boat with Spencer in it returned, but as "quite a wreck."[36]

By this time, John Canfield Spencer had learned where his son was, and intervened with what was likely a desire to "set him straight" through discipline—the kind of discipline that came from being at sea, not as an ordinary sailor, but as an officer. Now serving as secretary of war in the cabinet of President John Tyler, John Canfield Spencer arranged with Abel Upshur, the secretary of the navy, to have his son appointed a midshipman in the U.S. Navy. John's brother William Spencer was a captain, and Philip's older brother John Jr. was a purser. The whaleship's owner and master were informed by letter that young Spencer was the son of a prominent man, and was not to go to sea, and Philip was told to pay a local man $30 to volunteer to take his place. He wrote his father: "I have given you a good deal of trouble for a long time, but I shall give you no more trouble for some time."[37]

Sailing back to New York, Philip Spencer enrolled as a midshipman on November 20, 1841, and joined on board USS *North Carolina* at the Brooklyn Navy Yard. He was escorted there by his uncle, who left him under the supervision of passed midshipman and acting junior lieutenant William C. Craney. A "passed midshipman" had successfully passed the examinations for promotion to lieutenant, but actual promotion was a lengthy process in the pre–Civil War U.S. Navy. Craney was in that most unenviable of spots; he had to wait for a vacancy in the officers' ranks to get the promotion. So it was that he was the de facto but unpromoted "junior lieutenant" on a commissioned warship that would sail no more—a hulk moored for decades to serve as a "receiving ship" for new recruits to be trained aboard of, and lodging for officers and crew passing through the Brooklyn Navy Yard awaiting sea duty.

What happened next comes from Craney, who applied to work in Richard Henry Dana Jr.'s office to study law, on April 25, 1843, fourteen months after he quit the service in February 1842. Craney had entered the navy when, as Dana termed it, he was "quite young, and toiled up to a lieutenancy" in January 1832. As the "junior lieutenant" on *North Carolina*, he was on duty as officer of the deck when Captain William Spencer came on board with Philip. Introducing his nephew to Craney, Captain Spencer "asked him to assist the young beginner, by teaching him the ropes and looking after him in various ways." Craney was happy to do so, "pleased with the opportunity of befriending the son of the Secretary of War and nephew of an officer of high rank," and, as he later told Dana, he thought "it might be an advantage to himself if the young man turned out well."

However, poor Craney soon came to see that Philip Spencer "was a bad fellow and would make him trouble." He had allowed Spencer to use his stateroom—a great privilege for a newly commissioned midshipman, but Spencer "abused this liberty," keeping the lights on after the order had come for "lights out," "and by keeping bottles of

FIGURE 1.3 USS *North Carolina* at the Brooklyn Navy Yard

liquor under his bureau, with which he got drunk while Craney was in the city." After repeated attempts to get Spencer to see reason and behave, Craney reported Spencer to the ship's first lieutenant—the first officer—"but nothing was done to the son of the secretary."

Unaddressed, the behavior became worse. Spencer came into Craney's berth while the lieutenant was asleep and tried to take out a liquor bottle he had hid, waking up Craney, who ordered Spencer to leave; "I will go when I choose," said Spencer. Craney, still in his berth, ordered him to leave, "and then Spencer raised his arm and struck him a severe blow as he lay in his berth." Leaping up, Craney

pushed Spencer out of his cabin as Spencer fought to stay. The
ruckus brought the ship's officers, who told Spencer to go below to
the midshipmen's berths. But when the first lieutenant asked Craney
the next morning if he wanted to press charges against Spencer, and
Craney replied yes, as "the offense of striking a superior officer was
the worst that could occur on a ship," the first lieutenant said no,
and to drop it. "It will do you no good at the Department; Spencer's
friends are powerful."

Craney persisted in his complaint. Spencer was young and might
learn from the incident. But when Craney went below not long after-
ward to show the midshipmen the use of a sextant in navigating, he
was knocked to the deck in the chair he was sitting in when Spencer
came up from behind, grabbed Craney's uniform, and sucker-
punched him violently in the side of the face. As he fell, Spencer
tore off one of his shoulder straps that with a few stitches and a but-
ton identified his rank and ripped his coat. Craney quickly got to
his feet to fight but was held back by some of the midshipmen as
others dragged Spencer from the cabin. This was too much, too far,
an "offence which was punishable even by death if a court-martial
so ordered." Craney was also deeply embarrassed, as the lowest-
ranking officer on the ship had assaulted him, not once, but twice,
and this time in front of other officers. There are few secrets on a
ship, and so the attack was "well known to the ship's company," and
so for his own self-respect, "his own honor as well as a duty he owed
the service," Craney filed an official report on the two incidents.

All reports go through the chain of command, and the commander of the Brooklyn Navy Yard, Commodore Matthew Calbraith
Perry, sat Craney down, and advised him not to press charges. Perry
told Craney that Spencer had been given orders to report to the frigate *John Adams*, then about to sail for South America, and asked if he
wished to retract his report. Craney "instantly saw through this," he
told Dana. "Captain Spencer, finding Craney determined to report
his nephew, had written the lad's father and procured orders for him

to join another vessel, and prevailed upon Commodore Perry to retain the charges until Spencer should be sent away."

Craney refused, so the commodore said he would not send the report forward. That wasn't apparently good enough for Craney, who jumped rank and wrote the secretary of the navy directly. That didn't help. Craney "received a reply slighting the whole matter, as he thought, in an insolent and contemptuous manner." For his own act of insubordination, Craney was placed on suspension and not allowed to leave *North Carolina* while Spencer packed his sea bag and left for *John Adams*. Despite having spent "the prime of his life . . . in service," according to Dana, an indignant and embittered Craney resigned his commission. Dana, himself well acquainted with life at sea, was powerfully impressed by the story, and as he later wrote in his diary, as to whether Craney had exaggerated the story or not, "I never heard a story told in a more precise, methodical and calm manner."[38]

Spencer's time on the wooden frigate USS *John Adams*, a long-lived veteran of wars and actions, was brief. On *Adams*, he met Passed Midshipman Robert Rogers, who late in life (in 1890) wrote a detailed reminiscence of Spencer and *Somers*, which he served on after the events of 1842. Rogers had heard of Spencer before he met him, and his first impression came with listening to a heated, profane exchange with a Brazilian boatman who had landed Spencer at the quay in Rio de Janeiro, where he had sailed to join *John Adams*. Rogers got to know Spencer well, and they got along, despite the fact that "as a rule, he appeared to eschew an association with officers of his own grade. Mine was an unaccustomed face, and he found me unprejudiced by the generally unfavorable criticisms I had heard of him. He saw that I preferred to take my own measure of him rather than to accept that of others, which, especially with young people, and young people of a steerage afloat, are neither disinterested nor impartial, warped by professional jealousy and rivalry, independent of the truism that one officer is rarely just and judicious in weighing the character of another, when, too, judge and judged are contemporary and competitive."

Rogers noted that there were two sides to Phil Spencer; in his "rare normal moods" he was intelligent, educated, "had a fair acquaintance with the humanities," spoke "Spanish with fluency, even if it were, marred by grammatical blunders," as well as Latin and Greek, to which Rogers said he had "retained somewhat his hold" on, and was a "tolerably competent draughtsman." These all made him, "when he pleased," to be a "pleasant and plausible companion." But he also had an "an inbred, if not an inborn, inclination, I will not say to crime, but to the vicious at least. It was not by any means an eccentricity in the sense of whimsical, but a vagation so listless, indifferent, as to lead one to plunder a hen roost or a house." For Rogers, writing five decades later as an old man, "a more unbalanced, vacillating, and easily-corrupted nature I have never encountered," than that of Philip Spencer. He was also reckless, did not think ahead or consider the consequences:

> He was of that irresolute and arbitrary temperament which frets and rebels under the restraints and limitations society imposes for its own conservation. He would have resolved things to that primitive and barbarous freedom or anarchy which left all individuals free to do as they pleased, with no check beyond that interposed by other persons of a greater strength and prowess. To his licentiousness in that regard there would be joy and fascination in riding roughshod over the ways and methods law and ethics have been at such pains to establish and preserve. He would have infracted an ordinance simply because it was such, and because it interfered with that natural liberty which no human regulation had any right to repress or intermeddle with.

However, while for Rogers there was an "inherent baseness" in Philip Spencer, a family friend, upon hearing of Spencer's execution on *Somers*, wrote a friend that "I, of course, knew Philip only as friends know our children. I should as soon have expected a deer to ravage a sheepfold."[39]

When Rogers asked Spencer, one day when "he was normal, I mean, not warped by numerous nobblers" why as a "mutinous, insubordinate sort of fellow, constantly kicking against discipline, always in hot water," he had joined the navy. "I hardly know," he answered. "I wasn't a model boy by any means—pretty bad, lawless if you like that better, and my father, perhaps to get rid of me— perhaps to reform me—put me in the navy." When Rogers asked if he liked it, he shouted, "Like it! Like it! Hell, no. I hate it!" Instead, he told Rogers, "I think I would like to own a vessel outsailing anything afloat, with a crew who would go to hell for me; going where I pleased, doing what I pleased." *The Pirates Own Book* retained its hold on Spencer's imagination; he sketched portraits of pirates and of "sinister-looking crafts of the rover trim; and retreats lying in remote waters where plunder could be safely hoarded, and idle days spent in dalliance with captive beauties."

A "dipsomaniac, brutalized by the love of liquor, and too frequently intoxicated in places and under circumstances which showed how small was his self-respect and how indifferent to public judgment," Philip Spencer was "the most unpopular of the junior officers . . . and he was generally shunned." He "wandered into places where gathered the odds and ends of society, in and out of *cabarets borgnes* [bars with bad reputations], the reeky bagnios [brothels] of the Rue Sabôa, and with people who would not have paused to cut his throat, except that there was no need of it, for his maudlin and promiscuous hospitality impoverished him quicker than a sheath-knife would have done." His time on *John Adams* came to an abrupt end when he was seen by an admiral, as Spencer stood on the mole, in full uniform, screaming at an English naval officer "against whom he had a real or fancied grudge," and threatened to shoot him. Instead of resignation or court-martial, the orders came to send him home, to see what the secretary of the navy or his father would do with him. Rogers saw Spencer for the last time, after visiting friends to say goodbye on USS *Potomac*, then weighing anchor to return to the United States with Spencer aboard. "I remember well his valedictory.... He damned fleet and flag, the commodore and [Admiral] Wyman, rounding off with oaths and the threat to be 'even with them.'"[40]

When USS *Potomac* arrived at the Boston Navy Yard on July 31, 1842, Spencer was given one more chance. The small, overcrowded *Somers*, then fitting out on a voyage to Africa to deliver dispatches to the fleet on station off Africa, was to be his post. *Somers* would sail in six weeks' time, on September 13, 1842. Spencer was indeed trouble as well as troubled, and his time in the navy had only exacerbated his bad behavior. In another place, another time, he'd be labeled a delinquent, analyzed and found mentally ill, possibly schizophrenic, unaware and unafraid of consequences, and likely medicated.

The commander of *Somers*, Alexander Slidell Mackenzie, on learning Spencer was to be posted to his command, wrote to Commodore Perry to protest and ask for another officer, noting, "I have no respect for the base son of an honorable father."[41] That request was denied. *Somers* sailed on December 13 into history on a voyage that ended three lives and ruined many others. What exactly happened, why it happened, and if the executions were necessary dominated the attention of the United States, changed the history of naval training, and remain a topic of debate and fascination nearly two centuries later.

Chapter 2

An Unlucky Ship

Somers is a proud but unlucky name in American naval history. An act of Congress in March 1819 provided the rules for naming the ships of the navy and assigned that responsibility to the secretary of the navy. The biggest ships, of the "first class," would carry the name of one of the states. The "second class" were to be named for American rivers, and the "third class" were named for "the principal cities and towns." In time, these rules came to include steamships and merchant vessels acquired and added to the naval fleet. The rules also changed in time to allow naming naval vessels for notable naval leaders, battles, national figures, and the honored dead for their heroism or for their extraordinary accomplishments in the cause of peace.

With these rules in place and practice, in 1841, two small wooden vessels under construction by and for the U.S. Navy were named *Bainbridge* and *Somers*. The navy honored deceased naval hero and leader Commodore William Bainbridge (1774–1833), onetime commander of USS *Constitution*, "Old Ironsides," and a veteran of four wars, including two in the Mediterranean against the Barbary pirates and the War of 1812. The second honored Master Commandant Richard Somers. Somers (1778–1804) was the scion of a New Jersey family and schoolmate of future naval hero Stephen Decatur. Somers had a reputation as being somewhat of a hothead; he gained fame in naval ranks for fighting three duels on the same day in 1800 to "prove his courage."

The duels came in the aftermath of a joking remark made by Stephen Decatur. They were "warm friends and were in the habit of speaking freely of each other." On one occasion Decatur, in perfect good humor, called Somers a "fool," in the presence of five or six other officers. Somers thought nothing of the remark until several of the officers who heard it refused to drink with him. Decatur offered to clear it all up, but Somers was adamant. He challenged several officers to fight with pistols, scheduling each duel a few hours apart on the same day. They all accepted. Decatur agreed to serve as his second. The first duel ended when the other officer shot Somers in the right arm. The second duel ended when the other officer hit Somers in the thigh. Somers, bleeding and weak, had Decatur prop him up for the third duel. "This time, Somers hit and wounded his opponent. With that, the remaining duelists agreed that Somers was no coward, and the duels stopped."[1]

One ironic note on naming the two brigs for Bainbridge and Somers is that Bainbridge's misfortune indirectly led to Somers' death. The young United States, like other naval powers, was in the unenviable position of paying tribute to the Dey of Algiers as "protection" for American merchant ships that otherwise would be seized by the regional pirates of the Barbary Coast. A holdout from centuries of conflict between the Muslim and Christian states in the Mediterranean was the practice of seizure of ships and captives by both. On the principle that it was easier to pay tribute than fight a war, each year a U.S. warship would deliver the payment, but by 1803, American patience had worn thin, especially that of President Thomas Jefferson. On the president's orders, Bainbridge, in command of the thirty-six-gun frigate USS *Philadelphia*, was blockading the harbor at Tripoli (now part of Libya) when *Philadelphia* ran aground on an uncharted reef on October 31, 1803. As the crew cut down a mast, threw anchors, gear, and guns overboard to lighten the load and get *Philadelphia* off the reef, the tide fell, stranding the frigate further. There would be no escape.

Philadelphia remained stuck, surrounded by local boats from Tripoli that began shooting at the crew. Bainbridge gave the order to drill holes in the hull, flood the ship's powder, and leave little behind for their captors before surrendering. Bainbridge and his men were enslaved and locked in the fortress of Tripoli to await ransom. *Philadelphia*, refloated and hauled into the harbor, was renamed *Gift of Allah* and became a warship that belonged to the Pasha of Tripoli along with its officers and crew.

As a U.S. fleet arrived to resume the blockade, and plans were made to land Marines and take Tripoli. A smaller force, led by Decatur, arrived to make their way into the harbor and destroy *Philadelphia*. On February 16, 1804, Decatur and a volunteer force of U.S. Marines came in by night, using a Tripolitan ship they had captured, boarded *Philadelphia*, killed the crew guarding it, and set it on fire. Admiral Lord Horatio Nelson is said, perhaps apocryphally, to have called it the "most bold and daring act of the age." What now had to follow was to take Tripoli. Five battles on water failed to seize the port; Somers and Decatur and their crews fought hard from a fleet of small gunboats against the Tripolitan corsairs.

The decision to try another tactic took the captured Tripolitan vessel, now christened USS *Intrepid*, loaded it with a hundred barrels of gunpowder and 150 cast iron shells, and sent it in under Somers' command as a massive bomb to destroy the Tripolitan fleet at anchor during the night. With twelve volunteers, Somers and *Intrepid* made their way to the harbor entrance on the night of September 4, 1804. Before they got to the entrance to the harbor, which was protected by a mole, or seawall, guns on shore began firing, and *Intrepid* suddenly exploded. The dawn revealed burnt wreckage and bodies washed up on the beach. Whether *Intrepid* had been fired upon, or was about to be boarded and captured, leading Somers to blow it up to avoid capture, or the explosives on board prematurely detonated, Somers was heralded as both a martyr and a hero. One of Decatur's earliest biographers, Alexander Slidell Mackenzie himself, wrote that the belief at the time was that "the heroic Somers and his followers, seeing the

FIGURE 2.1 The ideal of a heroic U.S. Navy: Stephen Decatur at Tripoli

other boats around him, and no prospect of executing their project and escaping, resolved to prefer death, with the destruction of many of the enemy, to captivity . . . and determined to perish for their country, since that was the only service they could now render her, putting a match to the magazine, gloriously terminated their existence."[2]

The siege continued until a small group of U.S. Marines, with a force of Arab mercenaries, marched across the desert from Alexandria and captured the Pasha's fort at Derna. This gave the United States the leverage it needed to ransom Bainbridge and his crew and end what became known as the First Barbary War in May 1805. The end and the role played by the Marines is memorialized in the line of the Marines' Hymn "to the shores of Tripoli." Sacrifices and victory in 1805 notwithstanding, by 1807 the Pasha of Tripoli was back to his old ways. It would not be until after the War of 1812

BLOWING UP of the FIRE SHIP INTREPID commanded by CAP. SOMERS in the HARBOUR of TRIPOLI on the night of the 4. Sep. 1804.

FIGURE 2.2 The destruction of USS *Intrepid* off Tripoli

that the Second Barbary War, waged under the joint command of Bainbridge and Decatur, brought an end to the seizure of ships and ransoms. This was the legacy that inspired the secretary of the navy to name two new, unorthodox wooden ships for Bainbridge and Somers in 1841. Seamen are a superstitious lot, but the destruction of *Intrepid* and the death of Richard Somers and crew, or the capture and imprisonment of William Bainbridge and crew, were not seen as bad omens, but as sources of pride. And yet, looking forward with the hindsight of history, both ships were unlucky in their own way, and both were ultimately claimed by the sea.

Bainbridge and *Somers* were the products of a talented, veteran naval architect, Samuel Humphreys. Humphreys' father, Joshua, had designed and built the first frigates of the young U.S. Navy,

FIGURE 2.3 Richard Somers

including the famous "Old Ironsides." Following in his father's foot-
steps, Samuel had started work by supervising the construction of
naval ships, starting with USS *Philadelphia*, which he launched in
1799. Named chief constructor of the U.S. Navy in 1826, Samuel
Humphreys went in the next decades to design and supervise the
building of a wide range of wooden ships at a time of change in naval
architecture and naval warfare. Sam Humphreys, as his friends called
him, was a link between the old world of wooden sailing ships and
the rise of a "modern" navy. By the time Humphreys died in 1846,
still holding his official position, experiments in steam engines, pad-
dlewheels, and propellers and the introduction of iron heralded a
new age in naval architecture and war at sea, which was firmly set
into place by the Civil War that followed a decade and a half later.
But Humphreys was a master of the old school. When tasked with

designing new, fast schooners or brigs for the navy, at a time when the search for speed under sail was paramount, Humphreys drafted the plans for a sharp-hulled, small, hundred-foot-long vessel built for speed, working from earlier plans for two very successful naval brigs of 1834, *Dolphin* and *Porpoise*. At the time he completed his drawings with his assistant John Lenthall around 1839–1840, it was not sure what the two masts of the craft would be.

The brig rig—a "full" and more complicated rig with spars known as yards that crossed the masts, as opposed to the simpler gaffs and booms of a schooner—was what was finally selected. Sailing a brig was more complex, but better suited to the open ocean. Schooners also required skill to sail, but there was less to deal with when handling sail. The hull design was "fast and weatherly," meaning the hull as it cut through the sea was able to sail close to the wind.[3] These were naval craft built to be fast, and whenever possible, to avoid combat where a larger, better-armed ship would maul them. With their small guns, known as carronades, close-quarter weapons, and the naval equivalent of sawed-off shotguns, they were built to hit fast and low, and sweep an enemy's deck with buckshot or scrap iron and chain in the seagoing equivalent of a bar fight. Neither ship was built to fight per se—they were to run dispatches, delivering the mail and orders, and in the case of *Somers*, to be used to train young recruits to be seamen and for some, in time, to become officers. One drawback was that *Somers* was small and cramped, especially with a crew of up to eighty men and boys. The open deck swept from bow to stern; there was no elevated quarter or poop deck from which the captain and officers commanded the crew. Below decks, space was limited, with extremely tight living accommodations. The hold was lined with the anchor chain, stuffed with provisions and ammunition, and cabins were small, separated by thin-planked wooden partitions.

Rather than contract with a merchant shipyard, the navy built the two brigs in their own yards. *Somers* was laid down on the banks of the East River in Brooklyn at the New York Navy Yard, a venerable facility established in 1801 and an active and busy yard dedicated to the construction and repair of the navy's wooden ships. The yard remained active for 165 years, producing some of America's most famous warships, including the Civil War ironclad USS *Monitor*, the armored cruiser USS *Maine*, and the battleship USS *Arizona*. Civilian laborers and their families lived outside the yard's gates. *Bainbridge* was laid down and built at the Charlestown Navy Yard, outside of Boston, a facility also established in 1801.

On April 23, 1842, the *Brooklyn Daily Eagle* announced that "The U.S. Brig *Somers*, a beautiful vessel of 150 tons, and of twelve guns, was launched at the Navy Yard at Brooklyn, on Saturday. The brig *Bainbridge*, of the same size and model, is ready for launching at the Charlestown Navy Yard, and is only waiting orders from the Department." *Bainbridge* was launched in Boston on April 26. Those orders, after the decision on when to launch, included naming commanders and officers, and then rigging, arming, and fitting out *Somers*. On May 21, just a month later, the *Boston Post* reported that "Commodore McKenzie . . . has been detached from the steam frigate *Missouri*, and ordered to the command of the new brig *Somers*."[4] Alexander Slidell Mackenzie had already assumed command on May 12, 1842, when he officially commissioned it as the "United States Brig," not as the USS (for United States Ship), *Somers*. There were rules, and a brig, like a schooner, or sloop, was not a naval *ship*. That term was reserved for a three-masted, full-rigged vessel. Mackenzie was also not a commodore, but a commander, and he had not been born as a Mackenzie. In a snapshot kind of way, this somewhat inaccurate news snippet underscores what an enigma Alexander Slidell Mackenzie was.

Born in New York in 1803 to a merchant father, John Slidell, and Margery Mackenzie, he joined the navy at age of twelve in 1815 as an acting midshipman. The family was, in the parlance of the times, humble. His father, John Slidell, was a "soap boiler and chandler." The 1830 City Directory for New York lists John Slidell Sr. and Jr. at a "soap &c. manufactory, 50 Broadway."[5] The "old soap factory" belonged to John Slidell Sr., Alexander's grandfather, but in 1795, he turned the business over to his son, John Jr., Alexander's father. This was a humble and honest business, but not high-bred. Soap and candles were made by boiling tallow (beef fat) in cauldrons of saltwater to separate the fat from the scraps of meat, gristle, and bone. It was a grisly and redolent business, both in taking bloody, greasy chunks of bone and fat and boiling it for hours, and in the final product's qualities, described at the time by Charles Dickens as "flickering, strong smelling tallow candles."[6]

This was the working-class home industry that Alexander Slidell Mackenzie came from, a home that later in life as an officer and a gentleman he likely tried to forget. New York society most certainly did not; a 1911 gossipy reminiscence recalled a dinner party at which Alexander's brother John made what was perceived to be a tactless remark about the marriage of the sister of the woman he was seated next to. "Miss Fairlie regarded Mr. Slidell for only a moment, and then retorted: 'Sir, you have been *dipped* not *moulded* into society.'"[7] Would Alexander Slidell Mackenzie been acutely sensitive to such a "witticism" as it was phrased? He might well have flushed with shame, anger, or a little bit of both.

Alexander Slidell was one of several children in the large family of John Slidell and Marjorie Mackenzie. The oldest was John Slidell "Jr.," who was ten when Alexander was born. The other older siblings were his brother Matthew and sisters Jane and Caroline. Brother Thomas Slidell was four years younger, born in 1807. The family origins were humble, but Alexander's father and brother, going into business, had done well, his father as founding president of the Mechanic's Bank, established in 1810, and as president of the Traders' Fire Insurance Company. His brother John Slidell Jr. had as the oldest son gone into the family business as a partner. But in 1818, the family soap and tallow business, now known as "John Slidell, Jr. & Co." failed. Around the same time, John Jr. challenged popular theater manager Stephen Price to a duel in what New York society saw as sordid circumstances; the duel was allegedly over the favors of an actress both men were seeing. Slidell shot Price in the arm and badly wounded him. "It was the failure of his firm and the scandal of this duel that determined John Slidell, Jr. to go to a new State when there was an opening. He pitched upon New Orleans."[8]

There was not much to aspire to or inherit for the youngest boys in a working-class family of the time, so Alexander Slidell left home at twelve to find his way in the navy. Not much is known about his early career, as the records are incomplete, but in 1817, he was posted to USS *Java*, a frigate commanded by Oliver Hazard Perry, naval hero of the War of 1812, and from there to the brig *Enterprise*. After that, and his appointment as a midshipman in 1817, Alexander Slidell served on different ships as a young officer between long periods when he was furloughed or on leave. In the twenty-seven years of his naval career between joining the navy in January 1815 to when he assumed command of *Somers*, surviving records show that he was on leave for a total of nearly six and a half years.

This was not unusual for a peacetime navy of the era, especially for an officer in a system with a limited number of slots available for active sea duty. As a young midshipman, he spent two years on the frigate *Macedonian*. He was promoted to lieutenant in January 1825 after ten years as a midshipman, again not an unusual span of time for the period, and was ordered to the sloop *Falmouth* after two years on leave. As a new lieutenant, he was ordered to the sloop *Brandywine* for a few months, went on leave again, and then apparently returned and remained an officer on *Brandywine* for nearly two years before again going on leave. After returning from a two-year, three-month leave of absence, he was ordered to the ship *Independence*, remaining there as a lieutenant for nearly four years. After a brief leave of absence, and a promotion to commander, not yet a captain but available to command smaller warships, he was ordered to the newly completed steamer *Missouri* after its launch and fitting out at the New York Navy Yard. His tenure as first lieutenant was brief. Just a few months later, the secretary of the navy detached Mackenzie from *Missouri* and ordered him to New York to take command of the just-launched *Somers*.

FIGURE 2.4 Alexander Slidell Mackenzie

The Slidell family was not particularly well-moneyed; but while the Slidells were humble, they also epitomized the American adage of "self-made." In 1837, Alexander Slidell accepted an offer from his mother's brother to adopt the Mackenzie surname, as his uncle had no children to leave his estate to and wanted the family name to continue. This required a legal act on the part of the New York State legislature, as well as the navy's permission, and with both secured in early 1838, he was now known as Alexander Slidell Mackenzie. In 1835, he married Catherine Alexander Robinson, the daughter of prominent New York banker Morris Robinson, but the marriage of greater significance was his sister Jane's. In 1814, she married Lieutenant Matthew Calbraith Perry. At that stage in his career, Perry was not a commodore, nor was he yet the naval officer entrusted with taking a fleet to forcibly "open" Japan to foreign trade. He was the brother of

Oliver Hazard Perry, hero of the War of 1812, and Alexander Slidell Mackenzie's commanding officer on USS *Java*. Young Alexander Slidell, midshipman, joined *Java* not just as a junior officer, but as a member of the family. In 1842, Matthew Calbraith Perry was the commodore in command of the New York Navy Yard, and he had just succeeded in having *Bainbridge* and *Somers* built to test his new theory—educating young men to become naval officers.

Mackenzie, while a veteran officer, due to the large gaps in his service from furloughs and extended leaves, had never before been given command of a navy ship. It was a seemingly unusual choice for command of *Somers* until you consider that the U.S. Navy of 1842 *was* a family business. Nepotism ran amok. There was also a strong connection, forged not only by marriage but by words set to ink. That was because Mackenzie had not been idle on his furloughs and leaves of absence. He had traveled and written travelogues of his time in Spain and in Great Britain. Mackenzie also authored biographies of his naval heroes John Paul Jones and his former captain, and now kinsman by marriage, Oliver Hazard Perry. In this way, the son of the tallow merchant gained the respectability of a world traveler in an age when most people did not travel and sought to ingratiate himself with the naval elite. In 1829 he published *A Year in Spain*, followed by *An American in England* (1835), *Spain Revisited* (1836), *The Life of Commodore Oliver Hazard Perry* (1840), and *The Life of John Paul Jones* (1841). The young lieutenant was fortunate in his friendships in Spain, meeting and befriending the author Washington Irving, who later privately noted that he had "corrected" *A Year in Spain* "for the press and got Murray to publish in a very creditable style. It will give the lieutenant a complete launch in literature."[9] Irving wrote that the friendship was in part founded on Lieutenant Slidell's "masterly paper on the route of Columbus" that he wrote as a naval officer for Irving for the latter's work on Columbus. In 1850 a review of "Spanish literature" stated that "Mr. Slidell Mackenzie's *Year in Spain* enjoyed, and still enjoys an extensive popularity, for its vivid delineations of Spanish life and scenery."[10]

For Mackenzie, this was what at last set him apart, and distanced him, no doubt, from his humble past. People in nineteenth-century America cared a great deal more about the circumstances of birth prior to Horatio Alger and his enshrinement of the ideal of the "self-made man" as an American icon. His writing, and his status as an author, an officer, and a gentleman is what set Mackenzie apart from being a tallow monger's son, no matter that his father had in later life attained a good reputation as a businessman and as a "fine old knickerbocker," the term used in pre–Civil War New York to note that a man like John Slidell was among the city's business and social community. Knickerbocker is just a word, but it is the power of the word that can impact lives. Mackenzie knew this to be true, and where money would not work, being an author might bring recognition. It was also, conversely, the power of words that would prove to be his undoing. Mackenzie never learned the value of simply shutting up.

That began when he took up his pen to write about Oliver Hazard Perry, not so much as naval historian, but as a partisan in a family war against one of America's best-loved authors, James Fenimore Cooper. Cooper, best known for his *Leatherstocking Tales*, notably *The Last of the Mohicans*, published in 1826, drew upon his own brief service as a midshipman in the U.S. Navy to write *The History of the Navy of the United States of America*, published in 1839. A few sentences written about Oliver Hazard Perry's role in the War of 1812 Battle of Lake Erie, where Perry gained national fame and laurels of praise, stirred up criticism, especially from the extended Perry clan, who felt Cooper denigrated the reputation of the late hero by praising the actions of Perry's onetime second-in-command, Jesse Duncan Elliott. Perry and Elliott had bitterly vied for the laurels of victory for the Battle of Lake Erie, but when Cooper's book appeared, Oliver Hazard Perry could not take up literary cudgels on his own; he had been dead twenty years. Elliott was alive, but he had been court-martialed and placed on a four-year suspension without pay in 1840 after a scandalous cruise in USS *Constitution* under his command where he had disobeyed orders and abused his position for personal gain. This late-career punishment supported the Perry clan's belief in the character of Captain Elliott, so Cooper sharing the laurels between the two rivals posthumously was too much to leave unspoken.[11]

At the request of the Perry family, Mackenzie wrote a highly critical review of Cooper's book, taking specific aim at its depiction of the Battle of Lake Erie. Cooper, already suing other reviewers, initially held off, but in time engaged in a vicious war of words with Mackenzie that devolved not only into focused arcane arguments, but also personal insults and name-calling. The following year, at the request of Oliver Hazard Perry's son, Mackenzie wrote his biography of Perry. Friends of Cooper, but not they alone, complained of Mackenzie's "intense partisanship."[12] In response, Cooper wrote an essay to rebut Mackenzie's book in 1843. In his rebuttal, Cooper took special pains to call out Mackenzie's conflict of interest as a family member; the argument had taken on the ardor of a family feud.

While that war of words took place, Mackenzie gained his first command, aided and abetted by his brother-in-law, Matthew Calbraith Perry, who saw to it that his sailor-author brother-in-law was made captain of the newly launched *Somers*. On June 14, 1841, *Somers* "having been fully equipped, was turned over to the command of Commander McKenzie on the 14th of May instant, and her crew are to be put on board so soon as her officers report."[13] The officers soon arrived, as did the crew. At that stage Mackenzie, as captain, was supervising the last steps to ready his new command—his first, as noted—while they cleaned the ship and loaded provisions and gear. The other aspect was getting *Somers* ready to sail; the workers at the Navy Yard had set the two masts into the hull, both of them angled or raked aft instead of standing straight like a tree. After that, the yard workers' task was done; rigging the brig was now the responsibility of the new captain and his crew.

In addition to the hull's ability to cut through the water, the masts, yards, and sails were designed to generate speed. To be rated as an able-bodied seaman, a sailor needed to be able, on the darkest of nights, to grasp a line, know its name, and understand what purpose it served. This is the basis of the term "learning the ropes." On a vessel with hundreds of lines, this was no simple task, but knowledge came, often quickly, through practice and with direction provided by a friendly shipmate or less-than-patient or kind officer. Learning fast was essential, as missteps and mishaps could have deadly consequences whether sailing or fighting at sea in a warship. What transpired in this onboard education was the transition of a sailor—one who sails upon the sea—into a seaman, one who knows the moods and nature of the sea, how to handle a vessel, and in that, to handle it well.

The first paragraph in one of the earliest textbooks for seamen gives a sense of the technology and specific terms for lines and tasks:

> The Rigging of a Ship consists of a quantity of Ropes, or Cordage, of various Dimensions, for the support of the Masts and Yards. Those which are fixed and stationary, such as Shrouds, Stays, and Back-stays, are termed *Standing Rigging*; but those which reeve through Blocks, or Sheave-Holes, are denominated *Running Rigging*; such as Halliards, Braces, Clew-lines, Buntlines, &c. &c. These are occasionally hauled upon, or let go, for the purpose of working the ship.[14]

The technology, the rituals, and life at sea itself is a foreign domain for those who live ashore, but a specific and essential part of working and living as safely as one could on the sea. In the age of sail, this meant working the rig to capture the wind and drive the ship in the direction you needed to go. For a warship like *Somers*, this also meant doing so as fast as possible, especially when chasing or fighting another ship.

Key to that was rigging the masts, which was a complex job. Each mast was more than a single, rounded timber standing over a deck.

Four separate timbers, fitted together to tower above the deck, supported the yards, the rounded spars that hung perpendicular to the mast, and from which the sails hung. The lower mainmast, rising sixty feet from the deck, was topped by a wooden platform; here the main topmast was rigged and rose an additional thirty-six feet; this ended with another, smaller wooden "top," and there the next mast, the main top gallant mast, rose thirteen feet and three inches. Surmounting it was the main royal top gallant mast, rising twelve feet, two inches, and atop it was a four-foot pole. The total height of the mast was 130 feet, six inches from the deck. The foremast, also rigged from five separate timbers, stood 120 feet, nine inches off the deck.

Thick lines, covered with tar to help preserve them, were the standing rigging that supported the masts. The round wooden blocks that connected them were pierced with three holes through which the lines passed; they looked eerily skeletal, and were known to seamen as "deadeyes," and tarred lines were "shrouds." Up these lines the crew would rapidly climb, and then balance on foot ropes slung below the yards with bare feet, draping themselves over the yards to handle the sails, which meant kicking free the canvas or grabbing it with bare hands, pulling with forearm muscles while balancing on the soles of their feet on that line slung beneath the mast, high above the deck.

Other lines, the stays, connected the masts to each other, and stretched forward and aft. Everything was tied together, with the tension of the standing rigging and especially the stays helping keep the masts upright and the system balanced. The bowsprit, jibboom, and flying jib projected out from the bow at an angle; from it, sails rigged to capture the wind, the staysail, jib, and flying jib, aided both speed and maneuverability. A big spread of canvas, rigged aft of the mainmast on a boom and gaff, was another essential part of the rig. Additional sails could be added to gain more speed, running from the ends of the yards on poles that extended out, known as studding-sail booms. This added to the complexity of sailing a brig; they were difficult craft to manage and required a large crew to safely handle the sails.[15]

Captains were known to have their own views on rigging, and as his crew fitted out *Somers*, Mackenzie oversaw the rigging of the brig. Not everyone agreed with his decisions; First Lieutenant Gansevoort later commented they were "fitted differently than any I have ever known." But Mackenzie was the captain. Rigging the brig with the crew was also an essential step in getting the new vessel ready for sea, and understanding the captain's expectations of both how to sail it and how to repair it when something was damaged, either in a storm or through enemy action, was critical. While there were common aspects to rigging any sailing vessel, each rig, such as that on a brig, had its own nuances and differences. Like all tasks learned on a vessel, this was "before the mast," the seaman's term for learning while on board a ship, both on deck and aloft in the rigging.

As this rig was often hard to handle, there was the expectation that trouble would come. The extreme rake of the masts and the heavy use of canvas to give *Somers* speed had some old hands on the deck as well as on the brig muttering that *Somers* was "over-sparred and over-canvassed," and as "tender," meaning easy to capsize in a heavy gale.[16] So, too, was *Bainbridge*. Both brigs ultimately met their end when they capsized in storms and were pulled under the sea. *Somers* went over in a squall in 1846, taking a third of the crew, and when *Bainbridge* sank, two decades into its career, capsizing in a storm off Cape Hatteras in August 1863, it took all but one of the crew with it. An account of the loss noted that *Bainbridge* "was always considered a dangerous vessel and required great care to sail her on account of her being so taut, her masts raking very much."[17]

Once rigged, provisions were stowed; in all, about 120 tons of salted meat, biscuit, dried beans, rice, flour, water, and a variety of other necessities were placed in the hold. There too was the brig's magazine with the powder for the guns, and the heavy iron shot. The small size of *Somers* meant tight quarters for provisions and the crew. There was little unused space, and with spare spars and sails stored on the deck, in an area termed "the booms," there were two tight corridors, no more than a foot wide, that the crew had to pass through on either side of the deck. In the regulated life of a small warship, the old adage of a place for everything and everything in its place was a key rule by which a ship could function. Even the hammocks for the crew had their own place, bundled up in the morning and lashed atop the gunwales, occasionally wetted by the sea, and taken down and slung at night in the steerage below decks.

The crew, assembled by Mackenzie from the receiving ship USS *North Carolina*, and with his officers sent from other ships, included selections strongly influenced by Commodore Perry. *Somers* was the brainchild of Perry, who had earlier proposed sail training ships to offer instruction and hands-on learning away from the rough-and-tumble world of a large wooden man-of-war, an environment that social and naval reformers lamented was despotic, violent, and sordid. Perry sought to remedy that defect. He placed his brother-in-law in command of *Somers*, with a hand-selected wardroom of officers that included the commodore's son, twenty-one-year-old Matthew C. Perry Jr., twenty-seven-year-old Oliver Hazard Perry Jr., both Mackenzie's nephews by marriage, and seventeen-year-old Adrian Deslondes, the brother-in-law of Mackenzie's older brother, John Slidell, now a lawyer in New Orleans married into a local Creole family.

Non-family members included thirty-year-old First Lieutenant Guert Gansevoort, who was the older, first cousin of Herman Melville. Historian James Bradford notes that the nepotism of the eighteenth-century U.S. Navy "did not disappear but continued in the nineteenth century, exemplified by such 'naval families' as the Perrys and Rodgerses."[18] After *Somers*' first shakedown cruise, Henry Rodgers joined the wardroom as a midshipman. Rodgers, son of the recently deceased Commodore John Rodgers (1773–1838), a veteran hero of naval adventures and combat spanning the early history of the young U.S. Navy, was yet another distant relation of Mackenzie and the Perry clan. He had joined the navy as a midshipman in 1837. Henry Rodgers' older brother Robert Smith Rodgers was married to Sarah Perry, daughter of Commodore Matthew Perry. His uncle George Washington Rodgers was married to the commodore's sister Ann Perry, and Mackenzie's younger brother, William, had been a friend of Rodgers's seventeen-year-old brother Frederick and had died in an accident in 1828 with Fred Rodgers and another navy midshipman, Robert Harrison, when their boat overturned off Norfolk. The accident forged yet another, tragic bond between the families.[19]

Somers went to sea for the first time without Philip Spencer and other officers and crew on a shakedown cruise to Puerto Rico, then a Spanish colony with a growing trade with the United States. The shakedown cruise provided an opportunity to show the flag and reinforce America's interest in the island and its commercial opportunities.[20] Mackenzie's crew included older, experienced sailors as well as boys, officially rated as and known as "apprentices," who had come from the receiving ship USS *North Carolina* at the Navy Yard. They were on board to learn the ropes at sea while also schooling to become, in time, officers of the U.S. Navy with onboard lessons just like any other classroom, this one being on the brig and at sea. The shakedown cruise would test both them and the new brig.

Sailing from New York on Monday, July 11, 1842, *Somers* headed south-southeast, driving along the open Atlantic for some 1,400 nautical miles. In the midst of learning a new ship and new crew, tragedy came when apprentice boy John Farmer, stationed as a lookout, fell overboard. A second apprentice, Daniel McKinley, jumped in to save Farmer, who was younger than him and struggling to stay afloat. Mackenzie and his officers acted quickly, launching the brig's cutter, but Farmer was lost. The cutter's crew was able to rescue McKinley. Mackenzie was impressed by McKinley's "courage and alacrity."[21] This was the only outstanding aspect of the shakedown. From San Juan, Mackenzie took *Somers* back out to sea, retracing his track back to New York for a round-trip voyage of a month. The New York *Evening Post* reported on August 11 that *Somers* had "arrived last evening from a cruise, and last from Porto Rico."[22]

On the return voyage, Mackenzie wrote his report of the cruise to the secretary of the navy. In his assessment of brig and crew, he commented that a number of the apprentices were "far below mediocrity [in constitution and intellect]" and "wholly useless from their diminutive size," because, in his opinion, "Most of them are drawn from our large cities, and in many cases, as their names and phylogeny denote, they are the children of foreigners of the lowest class, brought up precariously in confined situations, their constitutions in many instances impaired by . . . diseases." What was needed, he felt, was to "procure apprentices from the country, from among the children of our vigorous, hardy, and independent citizens. . . . Healthy, robust, accustomed from their infancy to serve, and without that inveterate disposition to sulk, and those vicious properties conspicuous in many of our present crew."[23]

The New York that provided a number of the boys was a rapidly growing city of over 300,000 people, the principal port in America, and a business and financial center. Tremendous wealth resided in the choice neighborhoods. Elsewhere, industry—like the Slidell family's tallow-rendering soap and candle factory—intermixed with residential areas, rife with overcrowded slums, open sewers, disease, and crime. It was common to blame the immigrants who regularly arrived on sailing packet ships that had crossed the Atlantic. The Irish, fleeing economic hardship and starvation at home, were regular scapegoats as well as the primary recruiting ground for street gangs. The nickname "Paddy wagons" for the vehicles that carted prisoners off to jail was born at this time, "Paddy" being a nickname for the Irish; it was accepted by members of the community to describe themselves, but an insult when used by an outsider.

Alexander Slidell Mackenzie was "essentially a self-made man," in the words of one contemporary.[24] As a native New Yorker, and

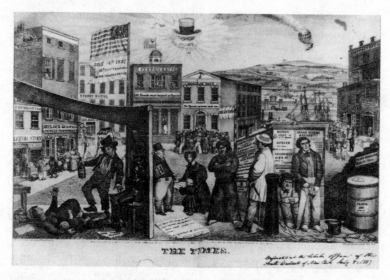

FIGURE 2.5 The rough-and-tumble New York of the era

as one whose family had embodied the American dream of success, the boys who boarded *Somers* for the shakedown likely roused his sympathies and his contempt. Mackenzie was likely both sympathetic to some of the boys for whom the navy could be a chance for success as well as prejudiced against those who did not measure up physically, intellectually, or morally. Returning from Puerto Rico, and preparing for his first operational cruise in *Somers*, Mackenzie weeded out as many of the apprentices as he could, returning all but seventy of them to USS *North Carolina*, and taking other boys from the receiving ship. As with the shakedown, older, more experienced men formed the backbone of the crew, teaching by example. By early September, Mackenzie had assembled 120 crew on board, 96 of them underage boys. The crew was divided into four categories or ranks: seamen, ordinary seamen, landsmen, and apprentice boys. The apprentices, based on their age, size, and abilities, were rated as either first-, second-, or third-class apprentices.

Philip Spencer, meanwhile, had returned to the United States. Ashore, Spencer wrote his brother Ambrose that he would stop in Albany to see him, "but shall not stop for more than a day as I shall apply for sea service immediately." Secretary of the Navy Abel Upshur, having read the charges against Spencer, had decided not to discharge him from the navy. He wrote Spencer, chastised him, and then returned his midshipman's commission and ordered him to sea, noting "what has past will be forgotten but if otherwise it will be remembered against you." With orders to report to Mackenzie on board *Somers* on August 13, 1842, Philip Spencer made his way back to New York and boarded the brig on August 20. Mackenzie "at once gave him my hand and welcomed him on board the *Somers*." Mackenzie quickly learned, however, "he had quite recently been dismissed with disgrace from the Brazilian Squadron, and compelled to resign, for drunkenness and scandalous conduct." Spencer would not fit in; the brig was already crowded, and Spencer was doubtless going to be a very bad influence. Mackenzie wrote Commodore Perry and asked that Spencer be removed. He was "a base son of an honored father" and Mackenzie bluntly stated, "I wish . . . to have nothing to do with baseness in any shape—the navy is not the place for it." *Somers'* tiny wardroom and its officers were a microcosm of the navy, and one that Mackenzie cherished. Spencer had to go "chiefly on account of the young men who were to mess with and be associated with him—the rather that two of them were connected to me by blood, and two by alliance, and the four entrusted to my especial care."

Philip Spencer, sizing up Mackenzie and the clannish wardroom, also decided that *Somers* was not the ship for him. The schooner *Grampus*, roughly the same size as *Somers*, was a twenty-year-old veteran of anti-piracy patrols. That included escorting U.S. merchant ships in convoys in and out of the West Indies. It had just the right reputation for the piracy-obsessed Spencer. In August 1822, *Grampus* had stopped and defeated a Puerto Rican pirate ship, *Palmyra*. *Palmyra's* captain and crew, pretending to be a legally sanctioned privateer taking ships from former Spanish colonies then engaged in their wars for independence, had ransacked American ships. *Palmyra* then had the misfortune to encounter *Grampus*, which ordered the other vessel to lower its colors and prepare to be boarded. *Palmyra's* crew instead fired on *Grampus*, which responded with a broadside that wrecked *Palmyra*, killed one man, and wounded most of the rest of the crew.[25]

The capture of the pirate ship and its seizure as a prize made national and international news, and Lieutenant Francis Gregory, *Grampus's* commander, was praised. Other actions and battles with pirate ships in later years only added to *Grampus's* fame. Stationed at Key West, Florida, *Grampus* also cruised the Gulf of Mexico and the West Indies, both pirate-infested seas as well as a battleground for privateers and patriots fighting for freedom from Spain, and in time, for Texans fighting for independence from Mexico. In 1840 and 1841, *Grampus* had shifted to anti-slavery patrols off Africa, and had just returned from that assignment to the Boston Navy Yard when Spencer arrived, in disgrace, on USS *Potomac*. Assignment to *Grampus* would mean a return to "pirate" waters for the schooner, and in a heroic, fighting ship, not a brand-new floating school. That had to appeal to Philip Spencer. But Commodore Perry denied the transfer, leaving Spencer assigned to *Somers*, much to Mackenzie and his fellow officers' dismay.

History would have been very different had Perry transferred Spencer to *Grampus*. Maybe he would have fit in, thrilled to be in pirate waters, or perhaps he might have run into trouble there, too. As for *Grampus*, assigned to the navy's Home Squadron in January 1843, it disappeared with all hands on or around March 10, 1843, thirty miles off Charleston, lost without a trace in a storm that struck the coast with ferocity. One account, from a relative of one of the officers, noted that after months of no news following the storm, it was clear that they had found "a dreary, reachless grave, in the cold, dark, merciless waters of the Gulf Stream."[26] With all provisions stowed, and with orders to proceed to sea on its first full cruise, *Somers* sailed from New York on September 13, 1842. The loss of *Grampus* would all be remembered later as yet another omen of impending doom, but instead of an entire vessel and crew, only Philip Spencer and two of his shipmates would end the cruise in a "dreary reachless grave" at the bottom of the sea.

Chapter 3

A Sailor's Life for Me

In 1840, the United States was a nation embroiled in dramatic change.[1] The nation was still in the grip of an economic depression that was the worst to hit the United States until the twentieth century. Two terms of a populist, authoritarian president and one term by his vice president had come to an end with an upset election that brought a new political party to power. The new administration faced a dramatic influx of immigration that was reshaping major cities. Political unrest, new religious movements, and rapid technological change and industrialization were transforming American society. All of this would have a profound effect on the navy, and specifically on the making of the crew of the *Somers*.

The nation was also expanding its territory. The thirteen colonies, then states, had grown into a sixteen-state union by 1800 and to twenty-four states by 1821, a move abetted by the Louisiana Purchase of 1803, but also by war and dispossessing native peoples whose ancestors had inhabited the land for thousands of years. American expansion was more than a move west to the Mississippi and north to the border with Canada along the Great Lakes and in Maine. The opening of the formerly foreign lands that would become the American Deep South made cotton as important to the American economy as oil would become in the twentieth century. There were more than economic consequences. The Louisiana Purchase, the War of 1812, and an eagerness to expand agricultural production, particularly cotton, into the new states of Louisiana, Mississippi, and Alabama had also expanded the scale and scope of

American slavery. This precipitated a national crisis that led to Civil War within a few decades.

The population of the United States, according to the Census of 1800, stood at 5.2 million persons. These numbers did not include indigenous Native Americans. By 1830, the population had more than doubled to 12.7 million; in that decade, approximately 143,000 people had immigrated to the United States. The 1830s added nearly five million more Americans; and that decade also saw immigration more than double, with nearly 600,000 immigrants listed in the 1840 census. In the 1840s immigration tripled.[2] The largest groups represented in this wave of immigration were the Irish and German speakers from the various Germanic states that in time would form Germany. Their arrival, in increasing numbers, dramatically expanded New York, the major port of arrival for immigrants. This was the social milieu from which Mackenzie would find his crew.

Steam technology opened the rivers and oceans to increased commerce, especially after 1840. So too did railroads, replacing earlier American improvements for internal trade and travel such as national post roads and canals. The most famous, the Erie Canal, aided the expansion of New York into America's principal port and largest city, and at that, three times larger than its closest rivals, the port cities of Baltimore and New Orleans. The early 1840s also saw the invention of the telegraph, a device that would dramatically expand the transmission of news by wire to newspapers across the country. It was that era's "instant news." The telegraph's importance in connecting Americans "virtually" was as dramatic then as the Internet and smartphones were in the late twentieth century. This would have a profound impact when the news of the *Somers* "mutiny" reached shore. Telegraph wires spread the story nationwide, and from there, abroad.

Another aspect of the changing American social landscape at the time of *Somers'* sailing was an awakening American reform movement born out of religious revivalism. There was an increased desire for religion and faith to be the means to solve social problems, and this brought major changes to American Christianity. The adherents to this vision focused more on an optimistic view that America could be transformed into a better society. Based on humanistic goals, the American emphasis of these movements was egalitarian, with the belief that each person had control of their own affairs. The various faiths, in the spirit of the times, embraced popular means of recruitment and worship through revivals and meetings, and inclusion of more women, and free blacks, with churches specifically founded for and by blacks, such as the African Methodist Episcopal Church. This was a turning point in America as it marked the rise of evangelical Christianity. Anyone could commune with God, and every American Christian bore the responsibility of bringing more people into the faith. Alexander Slidell Mackenzie piously believed in this tenet.

The concept of a personal connection to God that did not require a priest or minister also held great appeal to independent-minded Americans like Mackenzie. The religious fervor was such that swaths of the country were referred to as the "burned-over district," so-called "because the fires of religious zeal swept across it."[3] The heart of the burned-over district was Western New York, the home county of the Spencer family. "While not all Americans followed the movements, the concept of evangelical Christianity had, by the mid-nineteenth century, come to dominate American society."[4] Even with various denominations, differences in doctrine notwithstanding, Christianity was seen as having become "American" and not the faiths of Europe, and the United States was seen as a Christian country. Public institutions were seen as Christian. On a U.S. Navy ship like *Somers*, a captain was also the minister, all hands had Bibles, and religious ceremony was part of every day's ritual as well as a moral imperative. "This was not an age of tolerance, and liberty for all did not extend to any faith other than Christianity."[5] That certainly was Alexander Slidell Mackenzie's view.

Another core belief of Mackenzie's was that he was an adherent to the ongoing push of his times for social reform, specifically temperance, and the need for education. These movements had established associations for proselytizing, Sunday schools, foreign ministries, temperance, as well as larger movements dedicated to women's rights and the abolition of slavery.[6] Temperance movements in the 1830s reversed a trend of increased alcohol consumption. Between 1800 and 1830, American drinkers had reached a national average of five gallons per capita consumed each year, or more than double the modern intake in the twenty-first century. The temperance campaigns of the time by 1840 had begun to have an impact as annual consumption dropped, and targeted crusades, such as that intended to move from temperance to prohibition, took hold, especially on ships. Sailors, notes historian W. J. Rorabaugh, "had age-old drinking rites."[7] For the U.S. Navy, up until 1842, that daily ration was half a pint, or eight ounces of "distilled spirits." In drinking terms, that's nearly five and a half shots, which equals just over three ounces of pure alcohol. If you liked your sauce, then the navy was the place to go, even when the ration was watered down to diminish its effects. Reformers convinced the secretary of the navy to offer sailors who took the pledge to not drink a daily allotment of six cents a day to their pay. In 1842, the reformers succeeded in getting the ration cut to a gill, or four ounces. On *Somers*, Mackenzie cut it completely.

The changing times also introduced new institutions of higher learning, both secular and religious. Following the War of 1812, a handful of American colleges and universities were joined by over two dozen new schools. The same movement took former academies and refashioned them into the colleges Philip Spencer attended. Education was increasingly seen as key to success. Then came the Panic of 1837. It hit after two good years of economic growth. It also hit after the nation's first gold rush, when large deposits of gold were discovered in the Carolinas and Georgia. Its impact was as severe in its time as the Great Depression of the twentieth century. It lasted for eight years, during which banks and businesses closed, including nine-tenths of American factories; fortunes were ruined; and unemployment reached staggering levels. It was a time of despair, class conflict, and desperation. Two out of three workers in New York alone lost their jobs.

All of that opened the door for political change with the election of 1840. Diarist Philip Hone of New York, who had lost two-thirds of his fortune, noted in that year that America was "the whole body politic sick and infirm, and calling aloud for a remedy."[8] While many turned to evangelical Christianity and the new sects, the remedy chosen by the voters was electing the Whigs and ending the presidency of two-term president Andrew Jackson's hand-picked successor, former vice president Martin Van Buren. The Whigs came to power in 1840 with the election of William Henry Harrison, a veteran of America's decade-long Northwest Indian War (1784–1795). Serving in the House and later in the Senate, Harrison had been the Whig nominee in 1836, but lost to Van Buren. His running mate, John Tyler, a Southern plantation owner, slave owner, congressman, and senator, and a staunch supporter of states' rights, had been added to the ticket to get votes from Southern Whigs. While from an aristocratic Virginia family, Harrison campaigned as a common man, a frontiersman, and a war hero. Elected at age sixty-eight, Harrison was the oldest man elected to the presidency up until that time.

Whig ideals and conservative philosophy held that national governance meant a strong federal government and national unity with policies to promote industrial and economic growth, funding for infrastructure in line with those goals, and high tariffs to build up American industry and jobs. They had a general distrust of populism, derided Jackson as a tyrant eager to expand executive power, and generally opposed expansion of the country as a ruse to expand slavery for the economic benefit of a few.

Where stood Alexander Slidell Mackenzie with all of this? The forces of social and political change converged in Mackenzie's hopes for the brig's ultimate mission and purpose in the U.S. Navy. It was a naval vessel, but it was also a Christian ship with an educational mission, a moral purpose of taking boys off the streets, or from their dysfunctional homes, and molding them through instruction, experience, and the discipline of naval service to become officers and gentlemen. *Somers*, and life on board it, was to be an expression of the age, and not just a particular fervor of the captain. What ultimately happened on *Somers* came when those hopes were dashed, and not solely by Philip Spencer. Spencer in particular pricked at Mackenzie's sense of decorum and purpose in life, but the crew overall was to be an irritant. He was a man of his times and social class, and he well appreciated the status he enjoyed thanks to education, naval discipline, and service. The new administration in Washington was the right time for men like Alexander Slidell Mackenzie to assert the need for naval reforms to reflect social reforms, and to build a strong navy with moral, religious, and duty-bound officers and sailors on its ships.[9]

Mackenzie's time came in the aftermath of a crisis in presidential succession and a new secretary of the navy. William Henry Harrison died at the end of his first month in office in April 1841. Vice President John Tyler ascended to the presidency, but while the Constitution likely guaranteed him the office, Tyler was not fully accepted by all of Congress, who argued that the Constitution granted him the duties and responsibilities, but not the office of president, and even some in his own party in time referred to him as "His Accidency." Tyler was not popular with many Whigs, and had been added to the Harrison ticket for political expediency to gain Southern votes. With Harrison's death, Tyler now presided over a coalition cabinet allied to a party that did not support him. Tyler openly warred with Whigs in Congress. They expelled him from their party. After Tyler twice vetoed Whig bills, Whig supporters hanged Tyler in effigy and then burned it on the White House porch. The coalition soon splintered with the resignation of all the cabinet save Secretary of State Daniel Webster, who stayed because he was in treaty negotiations.

Tyler appointed a new cabinet, among them John Canfield Spencer as secretary of war. The elder Spencer served in that office until 1843, when he assumed a new post as secretary of the treasury.

Spencer's obituary described him as a "man of distinguished intellectual powers," but a type of man "seldom popular ... their passions, even that of ambition, are tinged with severity, and lean—for this is the vice of noble minds—to the love of power."[10] And yet Spencer was "never guided, nor seemed to guide the popular interest. His genius was not politics ... his nature was not lithe or supple enough to meet every changing breeze with the ready sail. . . . He was, in short, not a modern politician—his mind could not dispense with principles."

Also joining the cabinet was Abel P. Upshur, a Southern politician, replacing Secretary of the Navy George Badger. His younger brother George was a naval officer with twenty-three years of service who had advanced to a lieutenant's rank, and was a competent officer with sea experience that had included battling pirates off South America. Like John Canfield Spencer, Upshur was a lawyer and judge, but also a state legislator in his native Virginia. The Upshur family had settled on Virginia's Eastern Shore, where Abel Upshur was born in 1790, and worked their waterfront plantation, Vaucluse, with enslaved workers. While previously Southern politicians had been wary of extending federal power, men like Upshur had come to realize that a strong navy was in their interests.

These Southern "navalists" were "particularly concerned about slavery and the balance of power in the Gulf of Mexico, the Caribbean, and the near Atlantic" and who "saw the need for American defense of the seaboard—and the command of the oceans" as vital.[11] Tyler's selection of Upshur reflected his shift away from the Whigs to his own brand of Southern, pro-slavery nationalism. Taking office in October 1841, Upshur focused on improving the navy by reforms to the system that operated it, and by advocating for a larger and more modern navy. That included steamships and fast sailing ships, and more powerful weapons. Mackenzie and naval men like him found an ally in Upshur.

In his first annual report to Congress, a highly detailed document of greater length and scope than those of his predecessors,

FIGURE 3.1 Abel Upshur, Secretary of the Navy

Upshur plainly stated that "reform is necessary, in every part of the naval establishment," not only in terms of the size of the navy, modern ships, new technology, and higher standards for recruitment and training. Also needed was a reformed and revised code of laws, rules, and regulations at sea that reflected many of the reforms ashore. Left unchecked, the "evils" of the navy he had just inherited would "ruin the naval service." "What can be expected of a community of men, living together under circumstances tending to constant excitement and collisions, with no fixed law to govern them, and where even rank and station are imperfectly defined?"[12]

The victories of the navy against the Tripolitan pirates, in the War of 1812, and in anti-piracy cruises in the West Indies, Caribbean, and the Gulf of Mexico were a source of national pride, but had not brought Congressional appropriations, only peacetime budget cuts. Military-minded Andrew Jackson's administration had expanded the navy, and used it as a means to protect American interests, including gunboat diplomacy. Part of the expansion of the navy was also driven by new missions, such as patrolling the seas after the War of 1812 to suppress piracy in the West Indies and Gulf of Mexico, and to interdict the illegal slave trade from Africa. While American slavery remained legal at a national level, the Atlantic slave trade did not after January 1, 1808. In response to these missions, the navy built smaller, faster ships. It also experimented with the evolving technologies of steam and iron for use in shipbuilding. Among the proponents of a "modern" navy was Matthew Calbraith Perry. Perry personally supervised the construction of the steam-powered frigate USS *Mississippi* at the Philadelphia Navy Yard from 1839 to 1841, which with its sister ship USS *Missouri*, built at the New York Navy Yard, marked the successful beginning of the American steam navy.

At a basic level, the practical reforms for the navy reflected Andrew Jackson's simple philosophy that he reiterated in his farewell address as president in 1837: "We shall more certainly preserve peace when it is well understood that we are prepared for war."[13] Preparing for war at sea meant maintaining a navy and a marine corps in an environment and at a time when life in general was tough. Life on a warship was even worse: long periods at sea with little to no communication from home; hard labor in the dangerous environment of the open ocean; cramped quarters; an unappetizing diet of preserved meat and dried peas; lack of bathing and basic hygiene; and a strict discipline enforced with violence—fists, clubs, or flogging was the norm. Into this mix, seamen were issued "grog," or watered-down alcohol, in what today would be considered large quantities. This was the other focus of naval reform.

Unless a sailor had already "learned the ropes," and joined a ship's company with skills and experience, the progression in rating typically went from starting as a landsman, with little to no experience, to rating as an ordinary seaman after a year or so, and then advancing to an able-bodied seaman after two years' competent service at sea. There were no schools, nor training courses; all skills were learned on the job, with lessons enforced with all forms of discipline for mistakes. A particularly barbaric form, flogging, saw a man tied down, bare back, and a knotted "cat-o'-nine-tails"—a multi-tailed whip with each "tail" knotted—heavily brought down, repeatedly, bruising and then cutting open his back as the rest of the crew stood by in ranks to witness the punishment. The lack of education extended not only to seamanship, but also to the basics of a classical education, which was an essential need for officers as well for petty officers and sailors. William McNally, a former gunner's mate who joined the navy as a boy in 1829, writing on the "evils and abuses in the naval and merchant service" in 1839, noted that he had benefited from self-study and, once he became an officer, "the increase of my pay enabled me to purchase such books as I wanted, and in my state room I could study when I pleased; and nothing more was wanting than a teacher to direct my studies."[14]

That there were other problems, noted a reviewer of McNally's book in the magazine *Advocate of Peace* in 1840, "we defer other extracts concerning the *severity of punishments* in our navy, and respecting its tendency to produce a fearful amount of *intemperance and licentiousness*" [original emphasis].[15] McNally and other authors also made pointed references to naval discipline, especially flogging, and as historian Myra Glenn notes, their narratives "challenged the American public to view the recipients of abuse . . . as individuals with as much claim to their personhood and rights as anyone else," trapped in a system where the "power to punish was the power to control, subjugate those who were being disciplined."[16] In these decades of reform movements, accounts of naval and merchant marine floggings inflamed public sentiment. Readers of accounts in magazines or in books like Richard Henry Dana Jr.'s account of a flogging he witnessed as a seaman horrified the public. "A man—a human being, made in God's likeness—fastened up and flogged like a beast! A man too, whom I had lived with, eaten with, and stood watch with for months, and knew so well!"[17] Not only the brutality, but the absolute authority of a captain to order severe punishment, even the ultimate punishment, clashed with the ideals of those who advocated for the rights of the common man.

Without contesting the need for flogging, as the new secretary of the navy, Abel Upshur in his first report to Congress did strongly point out how the system could be abused and was abusive. Reform was needed, especially through applying a new code of rules, regulations, and laws. Reform also needed to include the moral betterment of the navy itself. This was underscored by another article in the *Advocate of Peace*, on the "moral character of the navy." It characterized service afloat as akin to being "kept like a criminal within the walls of a prison," and subjected to the "summary and barbarous practice of flogging on the bare back." The article drew from a report made to the Seamen's Friends Society by the Reverend J. C. Webster. According to Webster, while the treatment was deserved, what was at fault was the "nature of the system. It is one of the evils inseparable from a system of war. The system collects the worst class of men together. In the first place, what respectable man goes as a sailor on board a man-of-war? Many are adepts in crime before they go on board, and they are only rendered worse by their intimate associations."

Webster went on to note a lack of religious services, profanity, and how grog played a role in a debased moral character of the navy. But he noted the fault lay with the makeup of the navy's seamen, whom he classified as criminals, alcoholics, debtors, and "a class of youth, some with and some without parents or guardians, who were so refractory and disobedient, that they have been put on board our ships of war in order to keep the peace at home, and, if possible, to subdue their fractious wills." For the Reverend, "did I wish to be almost sure of sending a friend to perdition, I would put him at an early age into the navy. . . . Send a youth on board such a ship, and licentiousness, irreligion, and vain show meet him at the gang-way, and faithfully attend him, till, in nine cases of out ten, he becomes their relentless victim."[18]

The question of the moral code of the navy was a big one. It was more than profanity or irreligious behavior. The behavior of sailors ashore, frequenting bars and houses of prostitution, riled authorities and reformers alike. What happened on ships, however, also riled them, although what happened at sea—sex between men—generally stayed at sea as an open secret between seamen. While often referred to indirectly, it happened with frequency, likely on every ship. While not every sailor or officer participated, anyone and everyone who had served at sea knew all about it. When it was discussed, as in "intimate associations," or as logbooks indicate, "uncleanness" or "scandalous actions," it was blamed on shipmates. Physicians looked to other reasons. U.S. Navy Surgeon Gustavus Horner, writing on the diseases and injuries of seamen in 1854, offered his opinion that long periods of abstinence among crews led "persons of warm temperaments, free drinkers of wine and grog," to suffer from constant erections and torments that led him to suggest that giving crew access to prostitutes on shore leave might alleviate more than the medical issues he felt plagued some men on navy ships.[19]

But it was not a simple question of relieving sexual tensions or a lack of access to women. Some of the men did not want women. The world of a ship was where they could form relationships with other men in an all-male environment. Naval officers knew about it, but often looked the other way; some were also participants. The navy defined these relations as sodomy, technically a flogging offense. Sodomy was generally viewed as any "non-procreative sexual act." It remained a largely unspoken, but common practice on many ships in the British and the American navies. Mutual masturbation, fondling and kissing, fellatio, as well as "buggery," the term used at that time for sexual intercourse between men, were not uncommon. For reformers, especially naval officers in the know, this was particularly troublesome when it came to bringing boys to sea to become seamen. It was in this roiling atmosphere of social and political discontent, religious revival, and a code of silence that Upshur put forth a reform agenda. A ship like *Somers* would be a seagoing epitome of what a "proper" ship in the U.S. Navy in the age of reform should be.

One of the key advocates for reform was Matthew Calbraith Perry. Perry was at the head of a group of officers who advocated the reform of the navy's system of training. The standard practice,

FIGURE 3.2 A "boy sailor" of the U.S. Navy in a period advertisement

inherited from Britain's Royal Navy, was to assign young recruits to a ship, where, at sea, they would learn by example. While seemingly wise, it was less than perfect. Regular schooling, with all the requirements to become an officer through an understanding of mathematics, reading, writing, history, geography, and the classics, was often neglected. As well, the needs of the ship outweighed education. To become good sailors, then seamen and officers, the boys learned by doing. That was fine, but "to a busy ship and crew, the presence of raw recruits was often a hindrance, not a help."[20] One solution was to take older or unneeded vessels and turn them into receiving ships, where recruits would be housed and trained. One of those ships, the twenty-one-year-old ship-of-the-line *North Carolina*, moored next to the dock at the New York Navy Yard, was where Philip Spencer first went when he joined the navy. The others were USS *Pennsylvania* in Norfolk, USS *Columbus* in Boston, the brig USS *Pioneer* in Baltimore, and the schooner USS *Experiment* in Philadelphia. Starting in 1837, with a new system for training naval "apprentices" to become officers, a more formal education system began. For the nation to have a strong, professional navy to protect American trade, defend the nation at sea, and when necessary to project power, the old system needed change.

Perry, known as "Old Bruin," was forty-seven in 1841. He had worked hard to encourage proper training and schooling on USS *North Carolina*, but what emerged from that experience was the realization that simply being afloat on a ship that did not sail was insufficient. What was needed were more ships, with more opportunities to take aspiring young officers to sea to train them. Upshur was of the same mind. "There is no school for the sea-officer but the ship itself. The theory which he may acquire on shore, although a necessary part of his education, only prepares him to *begin* to learn what he is required to know as a naval commander. A small fleet, properly employed, will afford such a school to pupils enough to supply a large one."[21] There should also be proper naval schools ashore, noted Upshur, but this was a cause that Congress had deferred for

FIGURE 3.3 Commodore Matthew Calbraith Perry

some time, even though the army had its own academy for training officers-to-be at West Point.

It was then that Abel Upshur received a letter from Alexander Slidell Mackenzie that suggested that *Somers* and *Bainbridge* be selected as training ships for up to a hundred apprentices on each brig. Upshur agreed, as he believed that the experience would teach the boys and young men on board "the ropes." That old sailor's term for learning how to sail, however, does not reflect all of Mackenzie's agenda. They would also be floating schools in which a classic (but not classical) education would result in an officer corps that could read, write, understand math and navigation, and nurture a moral and spiritual compass. Mackenzie, a naval historian and author, would make an excellent commanding officer and de facto schoolmaster. The other aspect of the apprentice system was that many of the apprentices were being trained to become seamen and at best petty, not commissioned officers. Training before the mast was the sole purpose of the two ships, but they were also ships of war and were run as such, for part of the education was learning naval discipline and order. This was particularly important for the navy; the army had West Point, and the perception of the time was that the cadets there were young aristocrats, the sons of privileged and powerful families.

The navy had a bloated system where midshipmen were appointed through family connections—as Philip Spencer had been—but were not trained in the right environment. There was also the navy's larger problem. It was short-handed, and many of its recruits were either foreign-born, a problem for American nativists, or were, as Mackenzie complained after his shakedown cruise, unfit, former street urchins, or as one naval chaplain termed them, "the sweepings of the street." These boys, whether foreign or American-born, reflected the social distress left in the wake of the Panic of 1837; they were homeless children. Some brought aboard the traumas and the coping mechanisms of their very harsh lives. In ideal circumstances, reformers like Perry and Mackenzie saw *Somers* as a means to do more than provide a practical education at sea, but to also better them; another motivation was to remove young, impressionable boys from older, jaded men who could lead them astray with alcohol, tobacco, or sex.

The reality was that from the larger, real world, *Somers* was boarded by men and boys who reflected life ashore in all of its aspects. It also confined all on board to a small wooden vessel on a vast sea. Into this mix entered Philip Spencer and Alexander Slidell

Mackenzie. The high-born son was the subordinate to the son of the self-made man. One relished discipline and the power of the word; the other was a dissolute young man with a chip on his shoulder. In a doomed experiment, however well-intentioned, Spencer and Mackenzie were locked on a collision course on the high seas.

Chapter 4

A Fatal Cruise

Mackenzie, not yet tested in command, and *Somers*, not yet tested on an extended sea voyage, sailed from New York on September 13, 1842, bound for the coast of Africa with dispatches for the commander of USS *Vandalia*, patrolling the coast as part of America's effort to interdict the illegal transatlantic slave trade. *Vandalia*, when not at sea, would likely be found at one of the ports where provisions were available from the Canary and Cape Verde Islands south to Liberia. It was not a light undertaking: the coast was rife with slavers, some armed and dangerous; diseases, especially malaria, were rampant; and the coast had become a graveyard for sailors, whether serving on slavers or on anti-slavery patrols. Mackenzie sailed for Africa with a young, untested, and largely new crew. This would prove to be a key flaw leading to the voyage's terrible fatal outcome.

After returning from the shakedown cruise on August 10, Mackenzie had sent many of the apprentices back to USS *North Carolina* and embarked some sixty new boys, as well as four new seamen when one man deserted and three others were sent to *North Carolina*. New petty officers were appointed from the ranks of seamen on board, so that by the time *Somers* departed, five out of the eleven petty officers on board were newly appointed. Four new midshipmen also reported for duty, and the schoolmaster was sent ashore, leaving the task of formal education to Mackenzie. Mackenzie also had no second lieutenant assigned, meaning that Guert Gansevoort as his second officer had no other ranking officer to back him up in the chain of command. The lack of senior experience put some of Mackenzie's young men, in some cases untested young men in the wardroom, into positions of command that were intended for higher-ranking, more seasoned officers. Historian Angus Goldberg made the point succinctly. Three out of four of the officers in command of the various watches on the brig held acting ranks that were essentially promotions that demanded that each of them now assume a leadership role they previously had not been entrusted with. Even Mackenzie was learning as he went, as this was his first independent command of a warship.[1]

Another simple truth was that with 120 men and boys on *Somers*, there were too many persons on board. The usual allotment of crew for a naval brig was just over ninety officers and crew. Overcrowded, without enough older, experienced seamen or officers, and with *Somers* as a new, freshly tested ship with a tender, easy-to-break system of rigging, there was potential for trouble. *Somers* was not only overcrowded; it was a tightly packed shipload of teenage boys. A full quarter of the crew were sixteen or under, and nearly all of the remaining boys, in all two-thirds of the crew, were between seventeen and nineteen years old. Setting aside the concern of Mackenzie that many of his boys came from the streets, hormonal changes, different growth cycles, and what essentially is a rewiring of the brain's neural network in teenagers means that most of Mackenzie's crew, even if they were normal teenagers, were easily distracted, moody, horny, aggressive, and defiant.

Somers was essentially supposed to be a school ship, but it was also a functioning warship. Mackenzie would by necessity run *Somers* more as a warship than as a floating school, especially without an onboard schoolmaster. A warship ran on a rigidly defined, hierarchical, and strict system of discipline. Constant drills each day followed the rote method of teaching, and through it "even the most persistently stupid were taught their places and duties."[2] Those duties included training in the small arms—pistols and cutlasses kept in two locked arms chests at the stern by the wheel—by Master-at-Arms Michael Garty, a Marine assigned to the brig as its

FIGURE 4.1 The "sweepings of the streets" of New York

"policeman." On other warships, even small brigs and schooners, there was a small contingent, at least a dozen or more Marines, to enforce the captain and officers' rule over the crew. *Somers* had one, and for much of the voyage, he would be unable to fully perform his duties due to a persistent fever that confined him to his bunk.

Whether he had previously displayed these characteristics, Mackenzie overcompensated for his lack of backup by running *Somers* with a strict, quick-to-punish system. Discipline was physical, often violent, and inflicted in full view of the crew by Boatswain's Mate Samuel Cromwell. Mackenzie also assumed the duties of a ship's chaplain, as *Somers* was too small to be assigned that officer. Mackenzie, highly moralistic and a prig, thus became the de facto commanding officer, schoolmaster, and chaplain of *Somers*. He banned all alcohol except for the officers, banned cursing, and restricted access to tobacco. Not only did this not sit well with some of the street-wise boys on the crew; it also did not sit well with all of his officers. Facing a quiet rebellion, Mackenzie relied on standard naval discipline, harshly administered, by "coupling the bible with the lash."[3]

Somers had sailed not only without enough experienced officers and petty officers on a new, small vessel, but inexperience was compounded by *Somers* being a ship full of teenage boys physically and emotionally transitioning into men. Some historians have argued that Mackenzie was also unstable in addition to being inexperienced in command, especially on a ship ill-fitted to be both a training vessel and an active-duty warship on an overseas voyage. Mackenzie seemed to overcorrect for his lack of experience. He followed rules and regulations to the letter, supported by a wardroom of officers who were family or family friends, making his leadership team a tight, closed circle that would not check his behavior even if they had dared. They also had another reason to not confront the captain; he treated his officers, even family, with "more severity." No one would question Mackenzie or offer counterarguments to his judgments. That was the mood of the wardroom Philip Spencer now joined.

Spencer arrived aboard the tiny brig with a chip on his shoulder. He was met with a cold shoulder. The closed circle of the wardroom did not welcome him, and regardless of who snubbed whom, Spencer turned his attention to the petty officers, drawing large amounts of cigars, chewing tobacco, and smuggling alcohol on board in defiance of Mackenzie's orders. These he distributed liberally to a handful of men and boys. His first act after boarding was to buy a box of cigars from the purser and hand them out to the petty officers. Either he liked their company or wanted to curry favor. "He seemed to keep aloof from his brother officers altogether; he seemed to take great pleasure in the company of the crew." That included holding informal "concerts" with the crew by dislocating his jaw and drumming on it with his fingers while making "musical sounds." It may have been nineteenth-century beatboxing, a musical form that dates to the times with rural and African American origins, and not what would be expected from or by a young white male in 1842, especially a naval officer.

In these and other ways, Spencer fraternized with the crew. Fraternization, more publicly called out when officers and enlisted crew have sexual relationships, is more widely defined as *any* personal and/or business relationships between officers and enlisted crew, especially those that are "unduly familiar and that do not respect differences in rank and grade" and "violate long-standing custom and tradition of the naval service."[4] Spencer knew he was breaking the rules. When handing out cigars and tobacco to "the smaller boys," he told them that while it was against the rules of the ship, if Mackenzie wouldn't give it to them, he would. It wasn't that he liked the small boys; Spencer tossed coins on the deck to watch the boys scramble after them. That and the "gifts" were an open statement that he was better off *and* better than them.[5] Privately, to his friends, he called the boys "small fry" who "eat a large quantity of biscuit" but were "a useless article on board a vessel" that he would get rid of if it were his ship.[6]

Spencer also gravitated to those not fully welcome in society. That included the dark-skinned cook Edmund Gallia from Malta; "he used to lend Gallia his pipe to smoke." Spencer was also "very intimate with [Henry] Waltham, who was a Negro." The navy at that time was partially integrated, with a legally imposed limit capping the number of African Americans serving on navy ships at 5 percent of the entire crew. With African Americans serving on board, and as with society on shore, there were unspoken, racist rules that defined lines not to cross. Some were less so; South Carolina senator John C. Calhoun, an avowed proponent of slavery, proposed in 1842 to codify the navy's unwritten rule to only allow free African Americans to serve as cooks and stewards. Whether Spencer was not a racist is unknown, but he may well have been, and his liberality was a mask for using those marginalized members of the *Somers'* crew. The cooks were a source of additional food, and in the case of Waltham, the wardroom steward, smuggling alcohol on board before *Somers* set sail. Spencer had rewarded him with a frock coat and "bundle after bundle" of cigars.

At the same time Spencer made arrangements with *Somers'* black crew, he also befriended Samuel Cromwell and Elisha Small, both of whom had served on slave ships and made no secret of the fact. While slavery was legal in the United States, American participation in the transatlantic slave trade had been illegal since 1808, but enforcement was difficult and slavers had to be caught red-handed at sea. Spencer either thought enough of Cromwell, or wanted the burly boatswain to be obliged to him to the point of "loaning" Cromwell fifteen dollars, a large loan for that time and roughly equivalent to five hundred dollars today. His fellow officers watched Spencer engage in detailed conversations with the two men, noting later they found it, if not offensive, "unusual for young officers to inquire the history and adventures of the experienced seamen."[7] Whether that meant they saw Spencer as being a "fan boy" of the rough-and-tumble older seamen or again crossing the fraternization line, Spencer was not following the rules. Why should he? He was the son of the secretary of war, and he had gotten away with criminal assault on another officer, being publicly drunk in uniform, and insulting a foreign naval officer with no consequences other than being sent off to another posting before joining *Somers*. If the other officers didn't want to associate with him, then to hell with them, and to hell with the captain and the ship.

Spencer likely felt a pernicious sense of satisfaction in breaking the rules, but not in sight or earshot of Mackenzie. Every time he interacted with Mackenzie, face to face, observers noted he was quiet, deferential, and respectful to the point of obsequiousness. More than one witness pointed out whatever he said about Mackenzie below decks, "speaking very disrespectfully of him, when out of his presence in the steerage," changed when he came on deck and interacted with the captain.[8] Mackenzie as captain of a ship of boys was the father figure of *Somers*, and for Philip Spencer, he probably played Mackenzie as he played John Canfield Spencer: rebellious behind his back but with syrupy deference to his face. Behind Mackenzie's back, Spencer called him a "damned old humbug" and an "old granny." A humbug is a fraud, an imposter who doesn't merit their position. Spencer may have meant that, or have simply been using it in sailor lingo to express his sense that he was caught up in nonsensical circumstances that he had no love for. Richard Henry Dana Jr. wrote in *Two Years Before the Mast* in 1840 that when a sailor "feels that he is kept at work for nothing, or, as the nautical phrase is, 'humbugged,' no sloth could make less headway."[9]

Cromwell and some of the other men might have felt the same way about Mackenzie and his coterie of young officers on a ship of boys. Responsibilities for the older, more experienced men had to increase in these circumstances, and that had to rankle if not quietly infuriate them. It seems to have done so with Cromwell, who took it out on the boys from the start of the voyage. "He was very tyrannical toward them . . . when called upon to inflict punishment he would strike with all his might, as though it was pleasing to him to whip them. He whipped them hard, the same as though they were men instead of boys." Gansevoort later testified that Cromwell had "growled about the amount of duty," and that it was "damned hard usage."[10]

Somers arrived off the coast of the Portuguese island of Madeira and anchored in the harbor of Funchal on October 4. Strong winds had delayed the passage, so Mackenzie, eager to get to the African coast, left the same morning for Tenerife in the Canary Islands. Cromwell's dissatisfaction came out into the open. Gansevoort later recalled that "When I would give him an order, instead of executing it as he had done heretofore, he merely repeated it in a disrespectful manner, showing no disposition to see it executed."[11] Cromwell also focused his wrath on the captain. As the crew lowered one of the jibs, small sails forward of the foremast at the bow, the jib snagged on lacings installed under Mackenzie's supervision when the brig had been rigged for sea. "God damn the jib and lacing, and the damned fool that invented it!" Gansevoort was standing by and turned to Cromwell. "He knew the commander was the inventor of it, because I told him so before; I reproved him severely at the time, and he was disrespectful and sullen."[12]

Midshipman John Tillotson recalled that after *Somers* sailed from Madeira, Cromwell "would fly into violent fits of passion . . . would blaspheme outrageously; his whole character seemed changed; he showed an absent manner."[13] Cromwell also passive-aggressively confronted the brig's authority. When Tillotson gave him an order, he had to order Cromwell several times to do it before "he got up very leisurely, and repeated the order, and sat down again." It may have been disaffection, or the thought of a sixteen-year-old officer, nearly half his age, telling *him* what to do. At the same time, his manner toward the boys changed after Madeira; "he would let them pull and haul him about, he would be playing round the decks with them, he would let the boys large and small curse him, and he would take no notice of it."[14] After "damned hard usage," not being allowed liberty ashore weighed heavily on Cromwell, and his devotion to his duties—previously verging on the extreme—went away. The only consequences for his increasing insubordination was reproach, however. Gansevoort admitted at the court-martial that "my reasons for not reporting him were, that his services were very important to the vessel as boatswain's mate; we had no one to fill his place without crippling some other part of the vessel." Gansevoort then spoke the plain truth to the court. With a crew largely comprising inexperienced youths, and with an insufficient complement of officers, Mackenzie and Gansevoort had to make do, even if it bent or broke navy regulations. "Cromwell was chief boatswain's mate, and did all the duty of a boatswain" because *Somers* as a U.S. Navy brig was *not* "allowed a boatswain."

The necessity of keeping some of the senior crew as petty officers because their services were very important to the vessel did not stop Mackenzie from stripping Small of his rank of sailmaker's mate and returning him to duty as an ordinary seaman after *Somers* left Tenerife. Gansevoort was not a strict disciplinarian, and that extended to his own seeming love of drink; later criticized as an alcoholic, Gansevoort also had his own personal alcohol aboard, not hidden. He shared his wine and brandy with the other officers at their table, but like Spencer, also rewarded certain crew members with brandy. This was not in keeping with Mackenzie's temperance views and attempts to have a "dry" ship. Gansevoort may have been more the realist, as well as one who enjoyed a drink, while Mackenzie may once again have been an unseeing, unsympathetic, intolerant killjoy.

As *Somers* headed south to find *Vandalia*, the stops at ports to provision were brief, and never was the entire crew allowed liberty. When one watch was allowed it at Tenerife, and Daniel McKinley overstayed the allotted time, Mackenzie had him whipped. The "colt," a thin, three-strand whip, was used on boys, while flogging was done with a heavier cat-o'-nine-tails. The coltings were administered for neglect of duty, dropping a knife from aloft (potentially fatal for someone below), "disrespect," "insolence," for being noisy, blasphemous, spitting on the deck, peeing in your hammock at night, fighting, skulking to avoid work, or sleeping on duty. The floggings were done the same day for one boy who was a thief, and for another boy who received twelve lashes for "filthiness." The colt was not designed to break the skin, even when six to twelve lashes were laid on. But Cromwell administered these beatings with force, and so there had to be blood, although not as severe as the flesh-flaying pulping produced by the heavier cat-o'-nine-tails.

In total, punishment on *Somers* on this voyage produced 2,256 lashes to the backs and backsides of the boys and men on the crew. The fact that boys were whipped was not an issue in an age of strict discipline, and some of the coltings were for boyish behavior. Others were part of a rigid disciplinary system that punished, and did not forgive infractions—unless you were a favorite, or were needed, as was Cromwell. Another infraction, practiced by both the men and boys, was referred to obliquely as "uncleanliness" or "filthiness" in the logbooks of the time and as "shaking" to sailors. While some

FIGURE 4.2 Flogging a man on USS *Cyane*, 1842–1843

may argue the terms in the log meant failure to wash, in the parlance of the times, it was clear. It meant the "solitary vice" of masturbation. As the diaries of mid-nineteenth-century seaman Philip Van Buskirk note, one could shake it in the rigging, on sentry duty on a dark spot on deck, or in the hammock as it rocked and swayed with the movement of the ship. The punishment log specifically called out discipline for "being dirty at muster," or "being dirty and slovenly" and "having dirty clothes." Early in the log, only two punishments, for William Good and Stephen Swift, record that they each received twelve lashes each for "being filthy" on separate occasions. At Tenerife, however, ten of the crew were flogged for pleasuring themselves, perhaps to release tensions they had hoped would be alleviated ashore. All ten received between six to twelve lashes for "uncleanliness." After that mass whipping, no more punishments were handed out for filthiness or uncleanliness.[15]

The difficulty in being able to privately "shake" on the small, overcrowded *Somers* doubtless took away a means by which some of the crew had and could have coped with life at sea. After the mass whipping of the ten boys in early October after the Tenerife stop, if it continued, it was either exceptionally furtive or condoned. This added to an already unhappy ship. As the voyage progressed, tensions continued to grow while petty insubordination increased. Spencer was acting out his frustrations. One afternoon, he was near the bow as *Somers* approached land at Porto Praya, on another stop for provisions on the futile *Vandalia* "chase." Another midshipman asked him to "go up on the fore-yard, to look out for shoals and breakers." Spencer "said he was not going . . . it was the commander's orders; he said he did not care a damn." Mackenzie had not given him those orders. The other officer replied that he, as the "officer of the deck, had, if the commander had not." Spencer's reply was he didn't care. He was not going, and would not unless the captain specifically ordered him to.

When *Somers* anchored off and launched boats to go to shore, Spencer was ordered to go ashore in the second boat. James Wales, who was in the boat with Spencer, recalled that as they were climbing on to the boat, "I heard Commander Mackenzie observe to Mr. Spencer that he was not in uniform; Mr. Spencer went over the side muttering." As they rowed away, "after we had got some twenty or thirty yards from the brig the commander hailed the boat, and asked if we had the American ensign in the boat," Spencer yelled back, "that we had not got it, and then in a low voice remarked, not loud enough for the commander to hear him" that "he was goddamned if he was going back for it either, the damned old humbug [can] go to hell." It was, however, said "so that the boat's crew could hear it . . . he continued cursing the commander all the way to the shore." On another occasion, Spencer complained to William Neville that Mackenzie was "hard in flogging the boys," and called him a "damned son of a bitch."[16]

On yet another occasion, Spencer, noting that the captain's initials were A.S.M., remarked they would better reflect Mackenzie if the M. was exchanged with an S. Petty and petulant, Spencer was playing the passive-aggressive games of a schoolboy. That included "schoolyard" scuffling. Fellow midshipman Egbert Thompson recalled at the court-martial that Spencer "struck at me" on one occasion. "I warded off the blow, slapped him with my hand, then threw him down."[17] Gansevoort broke up the fight and had the two make up. Spencer also had a fight with Midshipman Tillotson. Again, true to form, Spencer landed the first blow unexpectedly as he had with Craney on USS *North Carolina*. By landing a "sucker punch," otherwise known as the coward or dog punch, Spencer was out of step with society as a whole, and especially within the navy. In mid-nineteenth-century America and Britain, "fair fighting" was a sign of good character, and learning to box, or practice the "art of self-defense," was the practice of "manly science" versus the assaults of "some ignorant ruffian" who "can commit assaults with impunity, without meeting with any punishment."[18]

After leaving the African coast and heading back toward the United States, Spencer's insubordination increased, as did Cromwell's and Small's. Mackenzie later recalled that when the officer of the deck gave an order, the three men were standing forward and "talking and laughing together." Spencer, who was on duty, should have repeated the order and in doing so ordered Cromwell, as the boatswain, to do the same and repeat the order to the crew. Two or three times the order was called out, but they "paid no attention to it, but kept on laughing and talking," forcing the officer to come forward and give the order directly to the crew. This was a breach of protocol, and Mackenzie, who was aft sitting on the trunk or skylight over the wardroom, known as the "round house," saw it and called Spencer to him. When he returned forward, "he was cursing the commander." Purser Wales asked him what the matter was. "The commander said I do not pay attention to my duty, and requested me in future to pay better attention; God damn him, I should like to catch him on that round house some of these dark nights and plunge him overboard, it will be a pleasing task to me.... I'll be God damned if I can't do it."[19]

Throughout his months on *Somers*, Spencer, while not a fully accepted member of the wardroom, had gradually fit in with a smaller group of men and boys. They were either his friends, or hangers-on to the son of a prominent man. Some of his associates were those who used to serve him and to lessen the burden of this voyage. A steward to rub his forehead when he had a headache, someone to wash his mattress, another to smuggle and provide him with alcohol. Like the boys who scrambled for his coins, or took his tobacco, they were not his equals. Some may not have been equals but with a different meaning or value to him. At the time of the "mutiny," as a list Spencer kept was passed around, the comment in the wardroom was that some "must be his chickens," or younger boys used as sexual partners. On a small brig, there are few secrets. There is nothing but innuendo, but on *Somers*, Spencer's peers believed him engaged in sexual activity. Thirteen-year-old John Cavanaugh, for example, the youngest on board, was a Spencer "friend," and historian Angus Goldberg suggests that Spencer had either befriended Cavanaugh out of pity or he was having sexual relations with the boy. If the latter, it may have been limited to "filthiness," the logbook term for masturbation, either in sight of each other or one masturbating the other. This was known as "going chaw to chaw," and the most popular place on any naval ship to do it was under the canvas covers for the booms amidships. That was where young boys met to service older men, often in exchange for favors, one of the few "private spots" on the brig. The activity had a name, the "boom cover trade."[20]

Another trysting spot was in the rigging, a favorite place to get away for conversation, to drink, or to have sex; on one occasion, Spencer was aloft, hidden partially by a sail at the foretop as Benjamin Green tattooed him, or as William Neville testified, "pricking India ink into Mr. Spencer's arm" with what Gansevoort suggested in his later testimony might be symbols of a more intimate relationship between the two.[21] Even the term "pricking," as Herman Melville and later scholars would note, had more than one meaning. Tattooing, which had spread among sailors in the eighteenth century after James Cook's voyages exposed his seamen to ornate Polynesian tattooing, had become an international practice by 1800, with about of a fifth of all American seafarers carrying at least one tattoo. The tattoo also had another meaning: it "branded" the recipient with "outsider status." But to be an "outsider" to some was to be an "insider" to others.[22] Melville, less than kindly, perhaps, noted in *White Jacket* that the navy in that time and place "is the asylum for the perverse, the home of the unfortunate. Here the sons of adversity meet the children of calamity, and here the children of calamity meet the offspring of sin."[23]

What all of this suggests is that caught in a world he has no love for, Spencer sought like-minded company to damn his circumstances, and damn the captain and the navy. He could have a life outside of the strictures of his appointment as a midshipman, and as an officer do it with a degree of impunity. By committing his prodigal son to the care of the navy and a schoolmaster captain father figure, John Canfield Spencer had left Mackenzie to do the parenting. But Mackenzie could effectively discipline Philip Spencer in no other way short of relieving him of duty and sending him ashore, something he could not do in this months-long chase to deliver dispatches to a commodore on a *Vandalia* that was always a port or two ahead, never to be encountered. And so *Somers* sailed on, quickly touching at each port before turning and heading back across the Atlantic to home, hoping to stop along the way at St. Thomas, in the Virgin Islands, where *Vandalia* was next likely to be.

It was then that Philip Spencer's games took a fatal turn. His conduct, hitherto petty and insubordinate, turned to dangerous outbursts. He ranted to his close circle of confidants about wanting to kill Mackenzie. Did he mean it? It may have been an expression of frustration, fired up by childhood memories of a fearsome father. What Spencer wanted most was to be taken seriously, even to be feared, rather than to have to answer to others he despised. But those statements of murder could not be taken seriously. As he did in college, when challenged by authority, he turned to those he chose as his peers and regaled them with tales of blood and murder. Spencer was fascinated by the deadly power represented by the brig, as well as by the waters in which *Somers* sailed. It was the heart of the illegal slave trade, a collection point for ships and men engaged in a despicable and lucrative business. It was a brutal, savage, and deadly business, and it clearly fascinated Spencer. Many of his questions to Cromwell and Small initially focused on their participation in the slave trade, as slavers on slave ships. He also, when ashore in Africa, spent his liberty visiting a Portuguese slave trader at his "factory," the term used for the barracoons, the pens used to hold captives before they were sold to European, Caribbean, and South and North American–based slave traders. After that visit, William Neville overheard Spencer ask Cromwell "if the *Somers* would not make a fine slaver."[24] The thought of joining the slave trade had appeal to some of Spencer's shipmates.

For others, it was agitation that *Somers* had chased *Vandalia* while on an ostensible anti-slaving patrol in those waters, and they could have had a more exciting and lucrative voyage. Apprentice Peter Tyson overheard two of the crew, Wilson and McKinley, say that they would "rather go in a regular slaving expedition" (not meaning being in the slave trade but stopping and seizing ships engaged in the trade as the U.S. and British navies were doing), "for there they had $35 per month and prize-money" for each vessel seized and sold. McKinley also said that when *Somers* got to St. Thomas, he would desert, "if he got a chance, and would go in a slaver; he said they were regular pirates in a measure." McKinley also received his own tattoo from Benjamin Green, both of whom clearly had been listening to Spencer's bloody tales. When asked if he tattooed McKinley with "the picture or likeness of a female pirate, from the Pirate's Own Book?" Green answered, "I pricked the picture of a female pirate, but it had an American flag to her." The portrait in the book was of Alwilda, a "Viking pirate" who dressed as a man; the image in the book depicted her in nineteenth-century attire brandishing a sword over her head. Spencer had also drawn his own picture, of a brig, that he shared in the wardroom with the other officers; "she had a black flag flying at her peak." If it was *Somers*, then the purser said, there

U.S. BRIG PERRY.   "off Ambriz. June 6th 1850."   AMERICAN SLAVE SHIP MARTHA.

FIGURE 4.3 The anti-slavery patrol in action: the U.S. brig *Perry* captures the slaver *Martha*

was a problem with one of the sails. Only later, and to some, would the drawing assume a sinister connotation.[25]

The topic of his favorite book fixated Spencer as he cruised on *Somers*. It may have started as imagining what could be if this fast, armed ship was his to command, with a loyal crew. It was an imaginary foray into a world where he was in control of his own destiny, a man on his own, doing what he wanted when he wanted. It was a game in his mind, and one that in trust he shared with his fellow malcontents. It also took firmer root as he began to script, in his mind and on paper, what would be required to take *Somers* for this purpose. At the same time he asked Cromwell's opinion on *Somers'* suitability for being a slaver, he also asked "how she would do for . . . a pirate?"[26] Another apprentice, walking by Spencer and Cromwell, who sat next to each other as Spencer with pencil in hand was bent over a piece of paper, overheard Cromwell say, "This would make a very fine piratical vessel."[27] Apprentice William Inglis also heard them talking, and said that Spencer told Cromwell that *Somers* "would make a fine pirate," and Cromwell answered, "Yes, sir; by clearing the decks of the boats."[28]

Spencer's discussions also included how he could take the brig with *Somers'* sole Marine, Master-at-Arms Michael Garty, when the brig was sailing between Madeira and Tenerife. Spencer told Garty he could take *Somers* with six men. "I told him he would not do it with three times six," Garty later recalled. "He said he would secure the captain and officers first, take possession of the arms and the crew, and when they saw his men in arms, he made no doubt that they would give in immediately." Garty shot back that the crew could "make a rush on him; there might not be more than six killed, and we could throw him and his six men overboard, and that he must think us a very poor crew, that he could take us off with six men. 'Oh, no,' says he, or something to that effect, as he went off."[29] Was this discussion plotting or hypothetical fantasy? It would later be seen in its most sinister aspect, especially after Spencer asked Garty which guns in the arms chest were always kept loaded, and where the key to the arms chest was.

What is not clear is whether Spencer actively plotted seizing *Somers* and turning pirate, or if he was playing, as he later averred, a "game." Did asking questions help him script his fantasy, or inform his plans? Was his drawing of a brig, but not *Somers*, with a black flag a visual step away from the near-impossible task of seizing *Somers* to finding a brig of his own to buy or take in St. Thomas after deserting *Somers*? Was his anger at his father, Mackenzie, and the system enough to see him through to murdering up to a hundred men and boys—if he even could have? On November 20, he told Michael Garty that he "was not going to be long in the navy" and that "he was going to have a vessel of his own shortly." Was that after a mutiny, or after reaching St. Thomas within the next two weeks' time?

Regardless of intent, Philip Spencer was firmly in dangerous waters; even if he was not plotting an active mutiny, his speech was edging toward sedition. What is stunning from the distance of the twenty-first century is why none of the officers communicated this to Mackenzie. Mackenzie was certainly frustrated with Spencer, and wanted *Somers* to be free of Spencer as soon as possible, but the sense from afar is that neither he nor the other officers took Philip Spencer seriously. That all changed on the morning of November 26, when Purser's Steward James Wales went to Mackenzie to report that the night before, Spencer had called him aloft, and there asked, "Do you fear death? Do you fear a dead man? Are you afraid to kill a man?" Spencer then confided a plan to seize the brig, kill the officers, and take *Somers* to the Isle of Pines, off Cuba, a pirate's lair, and turn the fast, armed *Somers* into a pirate ship. He told Wales that he had drawn up a plan, and had it rolled up in his neckerchief. The plan, he said, would start with a fight on deck:

> The affray would commence some night when he had the mid-watch; some of those concerned with him would get in a scuffle on the forecastle; Mr. Spencer would then cause them to be brought

before the mast; he would then call Mr. Rogers, the officer of the deck, to pretend to settle the matter; as soon as Mr. Rogers had got to the gangway, they were to seize him and pitch him overboard; they would then have the vessel to themselves; he would proceed to station his men at the hatches to prevent anyone from coming on deck.[30]

After opening the arms chest and taking out the weapons, Spencer would go alone into Mackenzie's cabin and murder him "with the least noise possible," and then go into the wardroom and steerage with some of his men and kill all of the officers. On deck, they would position two of the guns to be able to sweep the deck with shot, and then order the crew on deck. There Spencer "would select from among them such as would suit his purposes, the remainder he should cause to be thrown overboard," before sailing to Cuba and taking on

> one who was familiar with their intended business, and who was willing and ready to join them; this done, they were to commence cruising for prizes—that when ever they would take a vessel, they would murder all hands, as dead men told no tales . . . after taking from her that which would be of use to them, they would scuttle the vessel, leaving no traces of her; should there happen to be females on board, he would have them taken to the brig, for the use of the officers and men, using them as long as they saw fit; after that, to make way with them.

Spencer then gestured toward Elisha Small, who was standing nearby, and told Wales not to worry as Small was "one of us."[31]

Spencer continued, offering Wales the position of third officer, as well as money he would steal from the dead Mackenzie. Wales, thinking "it prudent to dissemble as much as possible in order to gather more of their movements," told Spencer he was in. As they got off the booms, Spencer followed Wales aft and spoke again; "If

I breathed a syllable of that which he had communicated to me, I would be murdered." Wales went below to tell Gansevoort, but Spencer was already there, and shooed Wales out. Wales, after a sleepless night in his own hammock, sought out any officer he could speak to the next morning. When Mackenzie heard the story, his first thought was that it was a fanciful tale by Spencer, who he felt had neither the means nor the backing to carry out such a scheme. He was said to have said, although it was later denied, that Spencer was "half crazy, or childish."[32] Nonetheless, Mackenzie had Spencer watched carefully, and finally approached Spencer as his suspicions mounted that there was something sinister going on. "I learn, Mr. Spencer, that you aspire to the command of the *Somers*?" "Oh, no sir," said Spencer, with what Mackenzie later described as a "deferential, but unmoved and gently smiling expression."

Mackenzie quickly laid out what Wales had shared: "You had a project to kill the commander, the officers, and considerable portion of the crew, of this vessel, and convert into a pirate?" Spencer denied murderous or mutinous; anything he had told Wales was "in joke." "You admit it." "Yes, sir, but in joke." "This, sir, is joking on a forbidden subject—this joke may cost you your life. . . . You must have been aware that you could only have compassed your designs by passing over my dead body, and after that, the bodies of all the officers; you had given yourself, sir, a great deal to do; it will be necessary for me to confine you, sir." Mackenzie ordered Gansevoort, standing nearby, to arrest Spencer. Gansevoort took Spencer's sword, more than a weapon but in naval ranks a symbol of authority and chivalry. Before they led Spencer aft and sat him down on the sternpost to chain him, Gansevoort searched Spencer's neckerchief for the paper Wales had been asked to feel the night before. There was nothing there. Mackenzie, standing nearby, asked Spencer "what are the contents of it?" It was an "old day's work," Spencer answered. "That is a singular place to carry a day's work; why should you carry it there?" Spencer shrugged and said he didn't know "except for convenience?" Pressed further, Spencer explained it was where he had kept his day's work on navigation, and had destroyed it. Gansevoort continued searching Spencer, rummaging now into his jacket and finding scraps of paper in his pocket. The list Wales had talked about was not on Spencer.[33]

This may have been the only time in a brief but troubled life that Philip Spencer was treated as a common criminal. It was by far the biggest scrape he'd been in, yet Spencer seemed calm, if not even bemused at what was happening. Marched aft to the very end of the ship and seated on the sternpost, in full view of the crew, who watched with shock at this unannounced, sudden turn of events, Spencer was asked to roll up his sleeves, and thick iron manacles were locked on his wrists. Now came double irons that shackled his feet at the ankles, linked by a short length of chain; Spencer could shuffle, but he could not run or even stride. Spencer was walked over the arms chest on the port side of quarterdeck, and seated on a camp stool. Gansevoort stood close by, pistol in hand. Mackenzie ordered his first lieutenant to put Spencer "to instant death if he was detected speaking to, or holding intelligence in any way, with any of the crew." At the same time, Gansevoort "attended to all his wants, covered him . . . when squalls of rain were passing over, and ministered in every way to his comfort with the tenderness of a woman."[34]

Night fell, and with it, the regular routine of changing watches and other duties. *Somers'* crew went about their work as if all was normal, but the men and boys were tense. The officers of the watch patrolled armed with cutlasses and pistols, roaming the decks to make sure the crew was going about its work and nothing more, fearful that an attempt would be made to rescue Spencer and seize the ship. Mackenzie was still not sure that Spencer had been telling the truth to Wales that there were co-conspirators aboard. Spencer, spinner of fanciful sea stories, rebel against authority, had again gone too far, this time in the crowded confines of a small ship where there were no secrets. Chained and manacled, as Spencer sat quietly watching the men on the deck at their work, he had to be thinking of what would come next, if it was like his earlier misadventures in which he'd arrive in New York under arrest, stand trial at a court-martial, perhaps, and then be free of the navy. *Somers* was three weeks' sail from New York and within a week of St. Thomas, and if the brig stopped at St. Thomas, there might be a chance to escape. Those who watched Spencer that night said he was calm and did not act like a man in fear of his life.

Chapter 5

A Hanging

When Lieutenant Gansevoort first approached Mackenzie with Wales' story, the captain's reaction was a slight smile. "It seemed to me so monstrous, so improbable, that I could not forebear treating with it ridicule."[1] It had to be Spencer spinning a wild tale, or playing an elaborate joke. Even so, it was, as he told Spencer, joking on a forbidden subject. Gansevoort also thought it was improbable, but before he had spoken with Mackenzie, Gansevoort had sought out Spencer on the deck to see if there was anything in Spencer's manner that suggested Wales' tale was true. When Gansevoort found Spencer, up in the foretop with Benjamin Green, getting his tattoo, Spencer had glared at the interruption for nearly a minute "with the most infernal expression I have ever beheld on a human face; it satisfied me of his guilt."[2]

With Spencer now manacled and shackled at the port arms chest, Mackenzie and Gansevoort turned to the question of co-conspirators. Spencer had told Wales that he had about twenty men and boys who were with him, but was that true? He was known to be friendly with Cromwell and Small, and Cromwell's insubordination and barely suppressed anger now assumed more sinister meaning. Had Spencer been in communication with Cromwell? No, but he had been with Small. This confirmed what Wales had reported; when Spencer shared his plot with Wales, Small had been close by, not hearing what was being said, but keenly interested. Spencer had spoken with Small in Spanish, and told Wales that he had said to Small that Wales was "one of us."[3]

Mackenzie studied both Cromwell and Small carefully on the morning of Sunday, November 27, during the morning muster of the watch. He later wrote that what he saw confirmed to him Cromwell was a risk, and that Small was close to panic over Spencer's arrest. "Cromwell stood up to his full stature, his muscles braced, his battle-axe grasped resolutely, his cheek pale, but his eye fixed, as if indifferently, at the other side. He had a determined and dangerous air." Small, however, "made a very different figure. His appearance was ghastly, he shifted his weight from side to side, and his battle-axe passed from one hand to the other; his eye wandered irresolutely, but never toward mine. I attributed his conduct to fear." Both had to be guilty, but Small had likely joined something that "was repugnant to his nature, though the love of money and of rum had been too strong for his fidelity."[4]

A search of Spencer's locker found a small razor case, empty except for "a small paper rolled in another; on the inner one were strange characters, which proved to be Greek." Midshipman Rodgers read Greek, so Mackenzie turned the papers over to him to translate. It was Spencer's list with, as Mackenzie read it, "well-known names among the crew. The certain, the doubtful, those who were to be kept whether they would or not, arranged in separate rows; those to do the work of murder in the various departments, to take the wheel, to open the arm-chest." The "certain" were Spencer, McKinley, Wales, and a man not on the crew, or least not by that name, of "E. Andrews." When questioned, Spencer told Mackenzie that Andrews was Small's real name and that he had shipped under an alias. The doubtful were several, including some whom Spencer had befriended: Wilson, McKee, Warner, Green, Gedney, Van Velsor, Sullivan, Godfrey, Gallia, and Howard. There were seventeen who were to be kept, either willingly or not; the only officer on the list was the doctor, Leecock.[5] Four of the doubtful had an X next to their names—Wilson, McKee, Gallia and Howard. Spencer had written in Greek that they "will probably be induced to join before the project is carried into execution. The remainder will probably join when the thing is done, if not they must be forced. If any one, not marked down, wish to join after it is done, we will pick out the best, and dispose of the rest." The second list had McKee taking the wheel, McKinley securing the arms chests, Spencer taking the wardroom, Spencer, Small, and Wilson taking the cabin, and Spencer, Small, and Wilson taking the steerage, all of this in "officer's country." However, one name not listed was Cromwell's.[6]

Sunday's religious service took place without any incident, but after that, the wind shifted and some of the crew were sent aloft, up the mainmast to add sail to catch the breeze and keep *Somers* driving forward. The main topgallant was ninety-six feet off the deck, and the main royal topgallant mast that topped it towered 130 feet. Ten stories up, then, men and boys were un-reefing and spreading the sails while adjusting the rigging to give the relatively smaller topmasts and their yards, now full of sail, enough slack to bend with the breeze as the wind caught the canvas. Instead of slacking the brace to loosen it, Small and seaman W. A. King hauled on the brace to tighten it; Rodgers shouted out, "Belay!" four times to make sure they heard him shouting to stop yanking on the line. King stopped, but Small "gave the brace a very heavy jerk," although other witnesses later claimed he yanked it two or three times, and the mast snapped.[7] It fell forward, carrying with it yards and sails, and would have crashed to the deck if it had not been tangled in the rigging. The lines held. One of the boys, Ward Gagely, had been on the highest yard, and he fell with it, but caught himself and climbed back up.

Cromwell, who had been sitting on deck patching some clothes, dropped everything and raced to the mast, climbing it, and other men and boys also sprang to as Gansevoort took command of the situation on deck. They unrigged the broken mast and yards, and lowered the wreckage to the deck to repair what they could. Mackenzie, watching the scene, said that while everything proceeded with "undeviating regularity," "to my astonishment, all those who were most conspicuously named in the programme of Mr. Spencer, no matter what part of the vessel they might be stationed, mustered at the main-top-mast-head." Was this a gathering of some of the more competent and motivated crew—ones that Spencer, if picking his imaginary "dream team," might have listed? Were they, as Mackenzie snidely noted, "animated by some new-born zeal in the service of their country" or "collected there for the purpose of conspiring." Mackenzie turned to look at Spencer, whose "eye . . . travelled perpetually to the mast-head, and cast thither . . . strange and stealthy glances." For the captain, this "confirmed the existence of a dangerous conspiracy, suspended, yet perhaps not abandoned." His suspicions grew when after supper the same crew returned to complete the repairs to the mast. Something had to be done, he thought, and so he "determined to arrest Cromwell."[8]

Mackenzie surrounded Cromwell with officers, including Gansevoort, who held a loaded pistol, which accidentally went off, wedging the lead ball into the deck. They then led Cromwell aft, sat him down, and Mackenzie began interrogating the man. Had he held secret conversations with Spencer? "It was not me, sir, it was Small."[9] The order went out to arrest and chain Small, who joined Cromwell, both manacled and double-ironed next to the starboard arms chest. Small confessed that he had been discussing Spencer's "plot" with the midshipman, but the question remained as to whether the "plot" was that or an older seaman listening to a young man's wild stories in exchange for the favors Spencer offered. After Spencer's arrest, apprentice Peter Tyson would later testify, he and another boy, Sears, went up to Cromwell and Small, who were talking, and asked why Spencer had been arrested. "For a supposed mutiny," Cromwell replied.[10]

Despite repeatedly being pressed to confess to conspiring to mutiny, both Cromwell and Small refused to confess. They were innocent. This did not stop Mackenzie from believing they were guilty, even when Gansevoort told him that Spencer, after the new arrests, said, "Cromwell is innocent. That is the truth, Mr. Gansevoort."[11] Mackenzie later confessed that Cromwell, as the largest, most powerful man on board, was a person to be feared, and so perhaps in that confession, the captain hinted at what motivated Cromwell's arrest; not the certainty of guilt, but the fear of what might happen if he *was* a plotter. Mackenzie told Cromwell "that he should take him home, and that he would be tried by the laws of his country; if innocent, he could prove himself so, if guilty, he would be punished."[12] As night fell, there were now three prisoners aft, guarded by officers with loaded pistols, and Mackenzie and the officers, all armed with pistols and cutlasses, watched the decks with growing unease. Some of them were near panic.

The boom, a heavy spar slung aft or behind the main mast, carried a large sail, known as the spanker, which could be raised or lowered to increase the amount of canvas, and swung from one side to the other to help the brig tack. The brace that held the boom in place snapped, and the heavy spar began to swing wildly. It was dangerous, but it could be handled, and the order went out for some men to come aft to help secure the boom. A trample of feet, and fifteen oncoming crew, pushed Gansevoort over and he panicked. "God, I believe they are coming!" he shouted to Mackenzie, and with a Colt pistol in his hand, he ran forward on top of the trunk, yelling at the men to stop, and pointing the pistol forward, he shouted that he would "blow the first man's brains out who would put his foot on the quarter deck."[13] The first man he saw and aimed at was Wilson, who was on Spencer's list. Mackenzie, meanwhile, had ducked down into his cabin, and emerged with a pistol in each hand. He stood behind Gansevoort, also aiming at his crew.

Midshipman Rodgers shouted out that he had sent the men aft to help secure the boom; Gansevoort shouted back that only a few men could come aft, but they were to watch themselves. No unusual movements, whatever they must do, do it in "their usual manner" or they would get "their brains blown out before they were aware of it." The boom was secured, but *Somers* was now a ship in the full grip of fear: fear by the officers of the men and boys, fear of the officers by the crew, and no one sure of exactly what would happen next. Thus began another sleepless night for many on the brig.

The mood, as far as Mackenzie and Gansevoort saw it, was "discontented and disaffected," "sullen and insubordinate," with groups of the crew "talking in a low tone," stopping or changing their tone when an officer approached, changing the conversation, or separating to return to work. Gansevoort later testified that "they were reluctant in performing their duty, slow in their motions, sullen and disrespectful in their manner."[14] It was time to demonstrate authority and discipline.

The next day, Monday, November 28, all hands were mustered to witness punishment. Steward Henry Waltham and apprentice Charles Lambert were brought upon deck to be flogged. Waltham's crimes were stealing wardroom brandy, and hiding three bottles of wine in a locker for Spencer. Lambert's crime was stealing a hat from Ward Gagely. "These were vile offences," and this was "not a time to bring the discipline of the vessel to a stand," so the two were "punished to the extent of the law."[15] Each man was lashed twelve times. It was only then, with men and boys arrested and chained, and after two beatings, that Mackenzie addressed the entire crew to share his thoughts on the "conspiracy" that he believed that even if the number of participants was small, it "was known to a majority." Mackenzie "commenced by explaining to them the general nature of the project of Mr. Spencer, studiously avoiding to excite any suspicions that I was in the possession of the names of those who were implicated. I was willing, in fact, that the worst of them should repent and hide themselves among the well-disposed portions of the crew." He reminded the crew that in three weeks' time, they would be back in New York. Had Spencer succeeded, he told them, a number of them would have never seen home and friends again, as he knew that Spencer and his co-conspirators intended to kill many of them, especially the "small fry." "Horror at the idea of what they had escaped from," "terror at dangers awaiting them from their connexion with the conspiracy," and not being able to return home "caused many of them to weep. I now considered the crew tranquillized and the vessel safe."[16]

The next day, the 29th, Waltham, his back already bruised, welted, and cut, was once again brought up on deck, and lashed twelve more times for hiding the wine. Mackenzie again addressed the crew, ordering them to "conform to the discipline of the vessel." He did not take the fatherly or schoolmasterly tone of the day before. He spoke as the master and commander of *Somers*, omnipotent and with deadly authority. The mood of the crew this time was also different. They were "far from tranquilized," Mackenzie felt, "the most seriously implicated," to him, or perhaps the ones who were like-minded with Spencer and Cromwell in seeing Mackenzie as a humbug, had begun "once more to collect in knots; during the night, seditious words were heard throughout the vessel, and an insolent and menacing air assumed by many."[17]

Paranoia gripped Mackenzie and his officers. Gansevoort spoke to the petty officers, who proclaimed their loyalty while insisting that *Somers* was "far from safe," with quiet conversations "among the disaffected; individuals not before supposed to be very deeply implicated, were now found in close association with those who were." Wales reported that he caught Charles Wilson, one of the men on Spencer's list, "attempting to draw out a handspike from under the launch, with an evident purpose of felling him" until Wales cocked his pistol and walked up to Wilson. Other men, also known to be friends or friendly with Spencer, missed the muster of all hands, among them McKinley and Green. The officers all observed what they believed were silent efforts by Spencer to communicate with some of the crew, including Cromwell, who was chained across the deck from him. Hands on a chin, half-smiles, looks were exchanged. Was it code? Or was it another example of how throughout the voyage Spencer had been "extremely intimate with the crew"? Mackenzie later wrote that he had "noticed the interchange of a passing joke, as individuals passed by him, a smile never seen but on such occasions, a strange flashing of the eye."[18] That eye was as out of place on his face as Spencer was on the brig. Was what was happening a silent set of bemused near-smirks, body language saying to those in the know,

"See what a humbug he is?" without pausing to reflect on the fact that Spencer had taken his game too far, if a game it was?

Mackenzie was losing control of *Somers*, either through a thwarted conspiracy, as he believed, or because his actions and command of the brig were evidence that he was in over his head. Mackenzie had also committed a cardinal sin for a parent or a schoolmaster; he over-looked disciplinary problems, as did his officers, until they grew so great that the only response was the contradictory, harsh imposition of punishment. More than two thousand lashes had been laid across backs of boys and men. If there were gatherings of the crew, and dis-cussions, they were focused on the actions of the "old man" and the officers, who were clearly afraid. All Mackenzie could think, in addi-tion to what to do next, was where, when, and how was this thing to end? His response was to escalate the situation on the morning of the 30th with more arrests. He started with names on the list, even though, as he would tell the newly confined, he had "only suspicions against them."[19] Charles Wilson, one of the disaffected and previ-ously flogged, was called aft, arrested, and chained. He missed mus-ter, and word had reached the officers that Wilson had a very sharp knife described as an "African dirk" that he had brought aboard that he would like to use or "put it into Mr. Spencer's hands," according to another crew member, Jonas Humbert. Wilson's knife, which he kept very sharp, so much so that he told Humbert it "would just as soon cut your throat," had "to do a great deal of slaughtering some of these days," and so Wilson was determined a threat.[20] Whether Spencer was playing a game or not, perhaps Wilson believed him in his "plot," and so, too, did Mackenzie and Gansevoort.

As the double irons were locked onto Wilson, Mackenzie called out, "Send McKinley aft." Daniel McKinley later testified that "I went aft; the commander and Mr. Gansevoort held pistols at my head and told me to sit down" next to Wilson.[21] Gansevoort told W.A. King, standing by with a handspike, to "knock out their brains if [they] should make a false move," or "knock them down with the first thing you can lay your hands on."[22] As to why McKinley was arrested, he was a paradox, a good seaman, a man of "admirable steadiness and command of countenance," but also at times disaffected and a man who had been flogged more than once.[23] He was next, said Mackenzie, because, in Mackenzie's opinion, McKinley was "the individual who, if the mutiny had been successful, would have made way with all his competitors and risen to the command." The manacles and double irons were locked on, and Gansevoort then ordered McKinley to "get on all fours and creep around the larboard side, as I could not walk."[24]

Alexander McKee and Benjamin Green were then called aft and also ironed. McKee was one of the crew whom Spencer spent more time talking with and gifted with tobacco; he liked Spencer, or at least well enough to answer when Spencer asked if he'd like to go to sea with him, that McKee would like to. Other than that, McKee had not stood out among the crew for any particular misbehavior, nor punished. He was on *the* list, and Spencer had "assigned" him to take the wheel; this is what landed him in chains. Green was also a discipline problem. He was "insubordinate," and enough of a favorite of Spencer's that the other officers ranked him as one of Spencer's "chickens," or sexual partners. As he was arrested, Green turned to Mackenzie and said, "I am very sorry for this." The captain answered with the threat that worse might come. "So am I, and I hope I will not have to touch any of you apprentices."[25] The four new prisoners were confined close to Spencer, Cromwell, and Small, aft near the quarterdeck, two of them chained aft of the #5 gun and the other two chained near the #4 gun on the port side. Mackenzie then returned to Small, hoping to get a confession and learn more about what he was facing. Spencer had gone too far with his game, especially in penning an improbable roster and plan for a fantasy mutiny that was admittedly damning. Cromwell and the others had gone too far in unchecked anger at the way *Somers* had been rigged, crewed, and commanded. And Mackenzie had now gone too far, seeing a conspiracy where none existed, even as he made a sympathetic nod to Spencer's "half crazy" childishness. He asked Small repeatedly if Cromwell was guilty. "That's a hard thing for me to say, sir," Small answered. Under relentless questioning, Small, aware that Cromwell had already told Mackenzie that Small was the one whom Spencer had confided in, told the captain that if "anyone aboard the brig" was guilty, then Cromwell was.[26]

At that stage, Mackenzie knew that *Somers* was a week away from St. Thomas in the Virgin Islands. He could stop there; a larger warship might be there, perhaps even *Vandalia*. While Mackenzie later wrote that he worried about the sanctity of the American flag, naval honor, and the safety of all, including saving the "unarmed of all nations using the highways of the sea from the horrors which the conspirators had meditated," he knew he needed to adopt "further measures for the security of the vessel."[27] He went into his cabin and, as a man of words, especially written ones, penned a letter to his officers. He asked them, as a "united council," to advise him on the "best course to be now pursued, and I call upon you to take into deliberate and dispassionate consideration the present condition the vessel, and the contingencies of every nature the future may embrace, throughout the remainder of our cruise, and enlighten me with your opinion as to the best course to be pursued."[28] It would later be noted that he had already reached the conclusion that Spencer, Cromwell, and Small must receive the ultimate degree of punishment he could apply as captain of the ship. He would execute the three.

That was in part because he knew Spencer's history of past breaches of discipline and official forgiveness. As the "son of a prominent man," Spencer would likely escape punishment if he reached shore alive. He also would say, though he later denied it, that Matthew Perry did not take Spencer off *Somers* when Mackenzie asked him to before the voyage. Because of who Spencer was, as well as what Mackenzie thought Spencer was, "made me very desirous for his removal from the vessel" before *Somers* had sailed.[29] Now he would do so by executing Spencer. Cromwell, the largest man on board, angry, prone to violence, and like Small, suspected of tacit or open support of Spencer's fantasy, also had to die, as did Small.

Gansevoort, Surgeon Leecock, Purser Heiskell, and midshipmen Matthew Calbraith Perry Jr., Henry Rodgers, Egbert Thompson, and Charles W. Hayes assembled in *Somers'* crowded wardroom. There, Gansevoort and the other officers called thirteen members of the crew in, one at time, to question them. It was not a formal court-martial but rather a "drumhead court-martial," the term used for urgent inquiries in the field, usually in battle, of grave offenses committed by officers. "Drumheads" were used to quickly come to judgment in urgent circumstances, and with near-immediate punishment without the possibility of appeal.

What was telling is that back in New York, when it was Mackenzie's time to be tried, the judge advocate trying him argued that all of the testimony provided to the officers on *Somers* in that wardroom was *not* admissible, as it was not the "proceedings of a lawful court." He did, however, "admit that the government at sea must of propriety be more summary than on land, and claim more allowances."[30] What happened in that wardroom over a total of only fourteen hours of hearing testimony and discussion is not how most Americans ashore would imagine justice to be; there were no constitutional rights there, no right to confront one's accusers, no cross-examination, no advocate for those on trial for their lives, and ultimately the judge was the captain, whose absolute authority he had delegated to this group of officers to enable him to administer his godlike power of life and death from the quarterdeck.

Spencer, Cromwell, and Small were not questioned, nor provided counsel from one of the officers to serve as their advocate. The court of inquiry into the actions of Mackenzie and his officers in New York, and Mackenzie's subsequent court-martial, exposed a flawed rush to judgment and a hasty execution fueled by personal dislike and near-panic. The evidence against Spencer was not cross-examined; Spencer, Cromwell, and Small did not have adequate representation; and even the damning evidence, a sheet of paper, written in Greek that listed possible co-conspirators, may have been only Spencer's attempt to form a sort of fraternity among the young men and boys on *Somers*. Or was it his fallback to his school days? Was he constructing an imaginary world that he could keep separate from others not in on his game through his knowledge of and use of Greek? Using his Greek, not all could read his thoughts or his fantasy-based plans. One aspect of the list that never got sorted out was that four names appeared on it that were not associated with *Somers'* crew. Were they aliases, or were they men or boys from other ships Spencer had sailed on? He confessed to Mackenzie that he had a "mania" for plots and had engaged in them on USS *John Adams* and USS *Potomac*.[31] Was the list from an older paper, a carryover as he refined his concept of a "perfect" ship and crew to be his own, and live a life as a pirate or a slaver? Whatever the real purpose of the "list" was, it was, at best, an imperfect piece of evidence.

What was also later revealed is that at least once, and probably twice, Gansevoort came to Mackenzie to discuss the case with him. This suggests that the officers' opinions in the wardroom, despite what was later represented, were not unanimous. Gansevoort later testified that he went into the council believing it was necessary to execute Spencer, Cromwell, and Small, saying he first felt the necessity "when we had made more prisoners than we had the force to take care of, and I was more fully convinced after the examination in the ward-room before the council of officers."[32] Later testimony also revealed that before the council met, Gansevoort had spoken with "the doctor, Mr. Perry, and Mr. Rodgers, and I think their conclusion was that they should be disposed of" before the council met.[33] Gansevoort also later agreed that he had freely shared with all of the officers Mackenzie's belief that the three men should die. Not only that, but that *Somers* could safely reach St. Thomas, and "immediate execution was necessary."[34] The whole matter was hasty; the doctor later testified that Gansevoort came in to the wardroom after talking with Mackenzie with orders to "get through with-it as quickly as possible."[35]

While the council debated, there were more arrests. Eight more boys and men were taken and chained: seventeen-year-old apprentices

Richard Hamilton, George Kneavels, and Eugene Sullivan; eighteen-year-old apprentices Charles Goldenham and Charles Van Velsor; twenty-one-year-old apprentice George Warner, twenty-two-year-old cook Edmund Gallia; and steward Henry Waltham. The last two were "colored," and in addition to Spencer liking them, racism played a part in the arrests, especially in an antebellum America fixated on the "horrors" of black rebellion. Andrew Anderson, appearing before the council in the wardroom, told them he was suspicious "about the niggers at the galley—I don't like them," but that "Cromwell could get anything at the galley—they appeared to like Cromwell there, he would very often take his pot and get coffee there."[36] Waltham, however, had also shown favoritism to Spencer because Spencer showed favoritism to him, and for that he had been flogged.

On the morning of December 1, the wardroom officers, led by Gansevoort, gave Mackenzie a letter stating that they have come to a "cool, decided, and unanimous opinion." Philip Spencer, Samuel Cromwell, and Elisha Small were guilty of plotting mutiny, had disaffected others in the crew, and believing that it "would be impossible to carry them to the United States, and that the safety of public property, the lives of ourselves, and of those committed to our charge, require that (giving them sufficient time to prepare), they should be put to death, in a manner best calculated as an example to make a beneficial impression upon the disaffected." Mackenzie was told about the verdict, and then handed the letter. He immediately concurred, and quickly gave orders "to make immediate preparations for hanging the three principal criminals."[37] The crew brought up 240 feet of rope from storage to cut into three "whips" or lines to hang Spencer, Cromwell, and Small, and Mackenzie went below to his cabin to change into full dress uniform. The officers, all armed, joined the crew on deck as preparations were made.

It was now 2 o'clock in the afternoon. Mackenzie approached Spencer, seated on a camp stool next to the arms chest, and looked down at him. He calmly, coldly, told Spencer that he was now going to die:

I informed Mr. Spencer that when he had been about to take my life, and dishonor me as an officer when in the execution of my rightful duty, without cause of offense to him, on speculation; it had been his intentions to remove me suddenly from the world in the darkness of night, in my sleep, without a moment to utter one murmur of affection to my wife and children, one prayer for their welfare. His life was now forfeited to his country, and the necessities of the case, growing out of his corruption of the crew, compelled me to take it. . . . If there remained one feeling true to nature, it should be gratified. If he had any word to send to his parents, it should be recorded and faithfully delivered. Ten minutes should be granted for this purpose.[38]

Spencer dropped to his knees and began to cry. He was not prepared to die, he sobbed, to which Mackenzie coldly reminded him that he was an officer and he set an example of dying with decorum "to the men he had corrupted." But he also told Spencer that "I know you are not" ready to die, "but I can not help it."[39]

Mackenzie then approached Cromwell, who was seated and reading a copy of *Knight's Penny Magazine*, an illustrated weekly from London dedicated to the "diffusion of useful knowledge," and if the latest issue of September 10, 1842, had made it aboard *Somers* before it sailed from New York, and Cromwell was reading it, the first article was on chivalry in the past, starting with "if ever an institution founded on so unnatural a basis as that of making war, or the art of destroying life, the pre-eminent object of living beings could have been permanent, it must have been chivalry; for certainly never was human institution better supported by all conceivable human devices." Or perhaps Cromwell was reading about Chinese boats, Newfoundland, coral, the nature and manufacture of velvet, or the geography of rivers, other topics discussed in that issue. Mackenzie interrupted Cromwell, who looked up. He, too, was going to die in ten minutes.

He dropped the book, and fell down on his knees and cried, "God of the Universe, look down upon my poor wife; I am innocent."[40] Spencer called out, "These are the last words I am going to say, and I trust they will be believed." "What is that?" Mackenzie asked. "Cromwell is innocent."[41] The captain walked over to Spencer, and talked to him in a low voice. He told Spencer that Cromwell never respected Spencer. He also told Spencer that some of the crew were laughing at him, one of them, Carpenter's Mate Dickerson, saying that Spencer was merely a "damned fool," while Cromwell was the "damned scoundrel." In Mackenzie's opinion, Cromwell used the *boy*, and once the mutiny was done, he would have either killed Spencer or made him his "secretary." "I do not think this would have suited your temper." With that, Mackenzie smugly noted, Spencer's face took on a "demoniacal look," and he said nothing more.[42] Mackenzie then walked over to Small and told him that he, too, was about to die. Small reportedly gave a slight smile, and when asked if there was anyone he cared to write to, "I have nobody to care for me but my poor old mother, and I would rather that she should not know how I died."[43] Mackenzie walked away, and Elisha Small looked over to Benjamin Green and smiled.

Spencer could not bring himself to write to his family, so Mackenzie sat next to him, on another campstool, paper in hand, and wrote as Spencer spoke; at that moment, Mackenzie was secretary to Spencer, but there was no mistaking what would soon follow. Historian Philip McFarland, writing in 1985, rightly noted how the "sanctimony of the interview makes for painful reading."[44] According to Mackenzie, Spencer had no message for his friends, but for his parents, perhaps with all the maudlin bluster a nineteen-year-old boy-man can muster, "I deserve death for this and many other crimes," as there are "few crimes that I have not committed," and "I have wronged many persons, but chiefly my parents." But his thoughts were not with his father; "this will kill my poor mother."[45]

Spencer's thoughts at this point can only be guessed. As the youngest child, he had probably sought to mitigate punishment from his angry, stern father by begging forgiveness rather than standing up to John Canfield Spencer. Standing before Mackenzie, another stern father figure, perhaps Philip Spencer's words were a cry for forgiveness, and for mercy. "I beg your forgiveness for what I have meditated against you."[46] *Meditated*. Was this contemplating, musing on, and even vocalizing a fantasy? Or was Spencer's use of the word acknowledgment of an actual plan devised for action? Or was it simply, "Yes, I did wrong, but please forgive me."

Mackenzie took Spencer's hand, shook it, "and assured him of my sincere forgiveness." But there was no bending Mackenzie from the path of righteous retribution. "I asked him if I had ever done anything to him to make him seek my life, or whether the hatred he had conceived for me, and of which I had only recently become aware, was fostered for the purpose of giving himself some plea of justification." Spencer answered, "It was only a fancy—perhaps there might have been something in your manner which offended me." Left unsaid, "You damned old granny, you humbug." He asked Mackenzie if the captain had "formed an exaggerated estimate of the extent of this conspiracy?"[47] Mackenzie's answer was an emphatic no. There was no mercy to be found here.

If, as Mackenzie said, it "had been possible to have taken him home, as I intended to do," it was not in John Canfield Spencer's nature "that his father should not have interfered to save him—that for those who have friends or money in America there was no punishment for the worse of crimes," and that even so, "this had nothing to do with my determination, which had been forced upon me in spite of every effort which I had made to avert it," and Mackenzie "regretted the dilemma in which I was placed."[48] As to how he weighed the consequences of executing the son of the secretary of war, Mackenzie, ever the moralist, convinced himself he was saving the Spencers from the disgrace that would come with a prolonged trial ashore. There was something here more than a lack of mercy; Mackenzie was the aggrieved party, and he bluntly told Spencer that it was because he was the son of a prominent man that Mackenzie was killing him now, lest Spencer escape "justice" ashore. "But are you not going too far," "are you not too fast? Does the law entirely justify you?" Mackenzie answered that Spencer had "not consulted me in making his arrangements" and that "his opinion could not be an unprejudiced one."[49] Spencer's view was prejudiced, as it was self-interested, but so too was Mackenzie's. This was not impartial justice. The time had now come to discuss how fast, and exactly how Spencer, Cromwell, and Small, the three "ringleaders," would die. Spencer wanted to be shot, as an officer; Mackenzie told him that all three would be hanged together. Please, Spencer asked, "cover my face." Mackenzie agreed, and a black handkerchief was brought to be tied over Spencer's face when they hauled him aloft. This "mercy" was also extended to Cromwell and Small. With that, Mackenzie turned away to see to the details of the execution.

The crew were all mustered, standing by the three whips, which were run up to the yardarms at the main mast's mainsail yard, thirty-six feet above the deck. The distance from the arms chests was not far, so the last steps for Spencer, Cromwell, and Small were few, although dramatic; Mackenzie was acutely aware of this, as he had staged it for maximum effect, mindful of, as he would later ask one of the crew, if they had "never been to the theatre or circus?"[50] Both Spencer and Mackenzie were masters of the theatrical. They went to the spots—Spencer alone to port, Cromwell and Small together at the starboard. As Spencer passed Wales, whose testimony of that night on the booms brought matters to a head, he stopped and extended his hand. "Mr. Wales, I sincerely trust that you will forgive me for tampering with your fidelity."

Wales said he did, and that he hoped God would forgive Spencer as well. He burst into tears as he said this, and around them, some of the boys and men also started to cry. "Farewell," said Spencer. Spencer continued, and came to Small, extended his hand, and asked if he would forgive him, "No, by God! I can't forgive you." Spencer asked again, and Small said, "Ah! Mr. Spencer, that is a hard thing for you to ask me; we shall all soon be before the face of God, and there

we shall know all about it." Spencer's voice wavered. "You must forgive me, Small, I cannot die without your forgiveness." Mackenzie
stepped forward and asked him to reconsider. "Do not go out of the
world with any bad feeling in your heart—forgive him." "Well, sir,
since you request it, I will," and shook Spencer's hand.[51]

Mackenzie, standing close by, also asked to shake Small's hand,
asking what Small had against him. "Nothing, sir; but I did not think
you would shake a poor bugger's hands like mine." Both men cried as
they shook hands. Mackenzie asked if he injured Small; what he had
done to merit Small's willingness to join a mutiny? "What have you
done to me, Captain Mackenzie? What have you done to me, sir?
Nothing, but treat me like a man." Ever sanctimonious, Mackenzie
told Small that he was doing this out of duty to the "flag of my country." He claimed that Small shouted out, "You are right sir, you are
doing your duty, and I honor you for it; God bless that flag and pros-
per it! Now, brother topmates, give me a quick and easy death."[52]

The three men, still manacled, stood as the nooses were placed
around their necks, the bristles of the hemp one last small irritating
itch before dying. Spencer asked Gansevoort if he could give the signal to fire the gun to signal the crew to haul on the whips and hang
the three; ever the dramatic, and setting himself above the others, it
should be his word, as the officer, that would hang him with the two
crewmen. Spencer then addressed his shipmates. He deserved to die
and his sentence was just and right. The whips were held by the crew
in three longlines; when the signal gun was fired, the men and boys
would run quickly with it to quickly haul the three bodies into the air,
hoping to break their necks or quickly strangle them in hopes of that
quick and easy death. Faces shrouded, they stood straight, feet on
the hammock rail in that brief eternity of waiting. But Spencer could
not say the word, though, and in that pause, Small asked if he could
address the crew, as did Cromwell. "Shipmates and topmates, take
warning by my example; I was never a pirate, I never killed a man;
it's for saying that I would do it, that I am about to depart this life;
see what a word will do. It was going in a Guinea-man [slave ship]

that brought to me to this; beware of a Guinea-man." He then turned to Spencer. "I am ready to die, Mr. Spencer, are you?" Spencer said nothing; Cromwell shouted, "Tell my wife I die an innocent man; tell Mr. Morris I die an innocent man."[53]

Spencer still could not give the command; Gansevoort went to him, and he whispered into the lieutenant's ear. Gansevoort walked to Mackenzie; "Mr. Spencer says he cannot give the word."[54] Mackenzie did not hesitate. "Fire!" As the carronade thundered, the crew, closely watched by armed officers, dashed forward, and the three bodies were whipped to the yardarm, struggling and dying. With them hanging above, Mackenzie mounted the trunk and addressed the crew. He offered a long soliloquy on the three dead "mutineers," explained his actions, including words somewhat to the effect of "Commodore Perry would not take the responsibility of removing that young man from the ship, but I have taken the responsibility of hanging him."[55] This was later denied, but it had its effect. He was the lord and master of this ship. He then called for the newly appointed boatswain's mate to "pipe down" the crew for supper. Before leaving, he called for "three hearty cheers for the flag of our country." With three cheers, an "electric moment" for Mackenzie, he felt a burst of pride and patriotism, but he also could not help to notice, with "pain, that many of the boys, as they looked at the yard-arm, indulged in laughter and derision." But Mackenzie would later note that he felt that "I once more was completely commander of the vessel."[56]

The bodies were lowered and laid out, and the crew were sent below for supper. A small group remained to clean and dress the three dead men, and prepare them for burial at sea by wrapping them in their hammocks, and placing Spencer in a makeshift coffin fashioned from two wooden chests. A thirty-two-pound cannonball was placed at the feet of the three, and they were ready to go into the cold, eternal embrace of the sea. A squall swept over the brig, lashing it with wind and rains and whipping up the sea, and then it passed. As darkness fell, Mackenzie, no longer executioner, but

FIGURE 5.1 Currier's color lithograph of the brig *Somers* with its hanged "mutineers"

now chaplain, read the funeral service by the light of battle lanterns strung along the deck. The corpses of Spencer, Cromwell, and Small were slid off a plank and hit the water; Spencer's coffin split, and his shrouded body was briefly visible before it began its fall thousands of feet down to the seabed.

The other twelve prisoners had watched all of this with fear, with no guarantee that on the next day they would not be next. Mackenzie calmly walked up and told them that they would not be killed; the bloodlust had abated, but close guard would be kept and if they made the wrong move, they would be killed instantly. McKinley cried when told he would not die that day. He and the others, ironed, were placed in large canvas bags that were lashed shut, and made the return trip home in these bizarre "quarters" to face whatever consequences they may find. For the officers, it was a nerve-racking voyage; still armed, standing long watches, they were pushed to the point of exhaustion as *Somers* raced for home.

On December 5, *Somers* arrived at Charlotte Amalie in the Virgin Islands to once again find that *Vandalia* was not there to rendezvous. Once again, it sailed on. Mackenzie and *Somers* would never catch the ship and fulfill the only non-training orders that the navy had issued. One tenet of this voyage, to deliver dispatches, was also now a failed task. *Somers* turned north, arriving at the Brooklyn Navy Yard on the evening of December 14. A small boat was lowered, and Oliver Hazard Perry Jr., with a letter for Secretary of the Navy Upshur, was rowed ashore. He took a fast carriage to Washington, DC. Mackenzie also landed, and arrived late at the family farm in Tarrytown. His wife greeted him, and blurted out that he looked awful.

Mackenzie only told her it had been a difficult voyage home, and that he was exhausted. He said nothing about what had transpired; he simply turned in to bed and went to sleep. In the morning, Mackenzie began a much longer, more detailed letter, again acting the part of a sailor-author, turning to words to lay out his case and justify his actions. Whatever metaphorical storm he had just weathered, he now faced a prolonged struggle not just for his reputation, but for his life. He had not just hanged three men for mutinous intent; he had hanged the son of the secretary of war. With that and other implacable enemies arrayed against him, now would come a crisis for Mackenzie, for the U.S. Navy, and in the opinions of some, for the nation itself.

Chapter 6

Controversy and Inquiry

The first news of *Somers*' arrival back in New York was a brief mention in the "Marine Intelligence" of the local papers on December 15: "ARRIVED U S brig *Somers*, Mackenzie, 8 days from Saint Thomas, and 31 from Liberia. Officers and crew all well."[1] The same issue of the paper, two columns over, advertised the Hamilton Literary Association's 1842–1843 lecture series, which had commenced with a November 17 lecture by Richard Henry Dana Jr. on "The necessity of a right life to a true appreciation of literature, and the influence of literature on life."[2] *Somers* lay off the dock at the yard for the next few days; no one was permitted to visit, and the crew remained aboard, other than twelve of the crew, now all ironed and transported to the nearby USS *North Carolina* to be imprisoned in less crowded circumstances. None of this was yet known publicly.

Following the hangings, and on the voyage home, Alexander Slidell Mackenzie's critical task, and one he felt best suited to perform, was to write his letter to the secretary of the navy in the privacy of his small, cramped cabin. While events were still fresh, this was his opportunity to lay out the facts, and explain his actions as the commander of a *Somers* in imminent danger. The letter, written on December 5, while still at sea, gave a brief account; this was followed by a second letter, finished and dated on December 14 as *Somers* anchored at last in home port, in which the commander apologized for not yet writing "a detailed statement of my cruise and of some other extraordinary events which have attended to it," but the weather had been rough on the final passage, and "during the last three days I have not had my clothes off, nor have I slept continually for an entire hour for the last fifteen days."[3]

Dispatched to Washington, DC, as soon as *Somers* touched the dock, Oliver Hazard Perry Jr.'s journey from New York to Washington with Mackenzie's letters was a long one, with the young officer reaching the capital on Saturday, December 17. The news broke immediately, inaccurately, and with dramatic effect. Additional details, many inaccurate, were published over the next days, even as newspaper editors made "vain attempts to obtain information of a more minute and reliable character than is ordinarily found in the first floating reports of startling events."[4]

Before any official proceedings, Mackenzie faced a trial by media that was waged in the nation's newspapers. While some papers adhered to a more cautious approach in reporting the "melancholy occurrence . . . and the consequences of good and evil to those concerned" because "the facts can only be truly and fully exhibited before the constituted tribunals of the country . . . it becomes therefore the duty, as we believe, as the conductors of the public press, to abstain, as far as practicable, from giving expression to opinions, until a full and fair investigation is made."[5] It was a noble thought, but then, as is now, they had to sell papers. The result, as Melville scholar and *Somers* Affair chronicler Harrison Hayford noted in 1959, "Do not expect to find . . . any accurate account of what happened" in the breaking news of December 1842.[6]

The first spate of news focused on a noble, gallant, decisive Mackenzie, of the plot including disrupting New York's commerce, the despoliation of helpless females and murder of all on board hapless ships, led by a wretched, troublesome "freak," Philip Spencer. Rumors of a letter deliberately planted in the press that *Somers* had sunk in a gale just before the "mutiny" "in anticipation of the success of their plot" by the mutineers, as well as another that Spencer had been cut down before dead and smuggled ashore alive in New York, fed conspiracy theories. Another false tale was that Spencer had stormed the cabin alone and armed, but had been defeated after a struggle.

Yet another was that Spencer and his co-conspirators were to rendezvous at the Isle of Pines with another naval vessel, the Republic of Texas Navy schooner *San Antonio*, which had gone missing and was feared to have been seized for piracy by its mutinous crew.[7] At the same time, the other emerging pattern in the news was the "division of opinion," in regard to the "necessity and legality of McKenzie's [*sic*] conduct... the officers would seem to have acted under a panic."[8] What ultimately emerged was a very public battle of words, waged by press friendly to the government, to the navy, and to Mackenzie, and by those who were not fans of any of the institutions or the captain of the brig *Somers*.

Among those was John Canfield Spencer, who did not wait long to publish a lengthy letter in the Washington, DC, paper the *Daily Madisonian*, on December 20. It was a forceful, angry document, as one would expect, but as one contemporary noted, it had all the hallmarks of Spencer's addresses to the court when litigating. He summarized the facts as best he could discern, noting that some of the details reaching the papers could only have been fed to the press by Mackenzie and his officers, but in that facts "so perverted, so exaggerated, and interspersed with so much surmise, and so much downright falsehood, so as to evince the deep anxiety felt to make sure of the first impression on the public mind."[9]

Spencer's recitation of the facts focused on (1) that the three were arrested on a charge of intended mutiny; that (2) "no disorder of a mutinous character appeared for the four succeeding days"; (3) that Mackenzie had requested his officers to give him their opinion on the "disposition of the prisoners," which was followed by the officers' interviews of crew without the three prisoners present or given the opportunity to "cross-examine the witnesses or make any explanation or defence, or to procure any testimony in their behalf," and then without "any form of a court, without even the obligation of an oath," the officers had recommended death for the three; and (4) that then, "when everything and person on board the vessel were perfectly quiet, after four days of entire security," Mackenzie hanged the three. The account of "S.," as the editorial was signed, was shocking to some, and welcomed by others. If, John Canfield Spencer asked, his son had told the captain that "it was all a joke," then this was "the mere romance of a heedless boy, amusing himself, it is true in a dangerous manner, but still devoid of such murderous designs as are imputed." The executions of Spencer, Cromwell, and Small, "against one of whom at least, there is not yet a particle of evidence," if proved to have been "the result of unmanly fear, or of a despotic temper, and wholly unnecessary," the law would have to prevail. U.S. law required a court-martial, "before which all parties are heard," and sentences were approved by senior officials. "This is believed to be the first instance in our history in which the law has been violated—the first in which prisoners—not of the enemy, but of our own citizens—have been put to death in cold blood."

Spencer closed by noting the remarks were made "not to excite prejudice, but to repel the attempt to create it. . . . Let justice be done; let it not be denied, because one of the victims was connected with a high functionary of Government, nor because another is unknown, and has not a friend or relation in the face of the earth. And let not wanton opprobrium be heaped upon the memory of the dead to justify the bloody deeds of the living." Prominent New York merchant and politician Philip Hone wrote in his diary the following day that the letter "is one of those strong, forcible documents" for which Spencer senior "is celebrated; fierce in style, rigid in argument," and it "certainly presents the subject of his son's execution in a light somewhat different."[10] None of this was good for Mackenzie; if "there exists any reasonable doubt of the absolute necessity for this awful exercise of power," Mackenzie "may wish sincerely that he had never been born to meet such a responsibility. A more dangerous opponent than John C. Spencer could not be found in the United States." At that stage, the navy announced that it was "not in possession of information sufficient to form a statement for the public eye," and so if there was no answer to the letter that upheld the necessity of the executions and the legality of his actions, then Mackenzie "is ruined past redemption."

The next day, on December 22, Secretary Upshur wrote to order Mackenzie to provide a more detailed report, and to deliver it post-haste. Mackenzie, ever the wordsmith, had been hard at work on what ended up being a thirteen-thousand-word narrative that would serve as his official report. While a report was needed, the document sent by way of Midshipman Rodgers to Washington was the wrong report to send. The narrative forwarded to Washington was a near-fatal mistake made by a man too proud of his skills as an author. The first rule of thumb in any report is to stick to the facts, plain and simple, and not to editorialize. Mackenzie not only editorialized. He sermonized. He moralized. He figuratively wrapped himself in the flag and held his Bible aloft. He included what he presented as transcripts of the dialogues he had with the men he had hanged. This was not just unfortunate—it was disastrous. Even his supporters and friends were horrified. One of his lawyers, Theodore Sedgwick, called it a "diabolical document" and lamented Mackenzie's conceited view "that he is a lawyer as well as a sailor and historian."[11]

Philip Hone's private reaction in his diary said it all: "well would it be for him" if Mackenzie's report "had never seen the light." Hone imagined John Canfield Spencer rejoicing in the document. "Oh that mine enemy should write a book!" Hone went on; "I have learned by experience and observation, that nine-tenths of all scrapes men get into are occasioned by writing or saying too much. Here is a document ten times longer than was necessary, written without consultation with any judicious friend." What had emerged was due to the "pride of authorship." Instead of a formal, factual report, there was a document "full of public details of trifling circumstances and irrelevant conversation," and "conceded so much that the confidence of his friends and the public . . . is shaken in the belief of the imperative necessity of the dreadful example which he himself felt called upon to make."[12]

Hone also felt that Mackenzie's observation that he had hanged Spencer because he would escape justice if sent ashore to be tried was a "national reproach, which even allowing it to be true, came with a bad grace from an officer in the American navy." Mackenzie's narrative was damaging, and remains so even after nearly two centuries' distance. It served as fodder for Mackenzie's critics for decades, and even now, neither presents the events nor the commander in the light he likely wished; however, if there was to be any "pride of authorship," perhaps Mackenzie would find solace in the twenty-first century that his account is the only detailed one that speaks to the events on *Somers* in 1842. What would pain the commander is how his narrative was received; he claimed to write fact, but some saw it as tinged if not tainted with an element of fiction. Hone noted that even when Mackenzie was writing nonfiction, as was the case with his first book, *A Year in Spain*, "which gave him some reputation as an author . . . he disdained to take advice in regard either to the matter or the manner of the narrative." The official report "in this particular . . . is a failure; it will add nothing to his literary renown." Hone was not an enemy of Mackenzie's, and he watched the inquiries and court-martial unfold with interest and a hope that the outcome was not injurious to the country he loved. "I trust he will stand justified before God and his country, not-withstanding his ill-judged report."

As the mood in the press darkened, Abel Upshur ordered a formal court of inquiry to be held as quickly as it could be convened in New York, and appointed Captain Charles Stewart, Commodore Alexander J. Dallas, and Commodore Jacob Jones as members of the court, with U.S. Attorney for the Southern District of New York Ogden Hoffman as the judge advocate who would present the matter to the senior officers who made up the tribunal. Witnesses would be called, and they could be and were cross-examined by the court and by Mackenzie. The inquiry was held aboard the station ship USS *North Carolina* in the Navy Yard, convening on December 28, just two weeks after *Somers'* return. It was a public affair, open to even the press, who followed it closely and published transcripts taken by reporters hastily scribbling their notes in the crowded confines of the captain's cabin. Richard Henry Dana Jr., who visited the court onboard, described the close quarters in a letter to a friend:

> A long table filled the room. On one side of it sat the three com-
> manders who compose the court; Mr. Mackenzie sat at one end,
> Mr. Perry (the witness under examination) stood at the other end;
> and opposite the court sat the clerk and Mr. Hoffman, the judge
> advocate. There were a number of auditors, and the reporters of the
> principal papers had a table to themselves.[13]

Captain Stewart, the presiding officer, was a sixty-four-year-old veteran who had served in the navy since 1798 as a nineteen-year-old lieutenant. A battle-hardened veteran of the War of 1812, his commands included USS *Constitution*, "Old Ironsides," and at the time of the court of inquiry, he was one of the most senior officers in the U.S. Navy and commander of the navy's Home Squadron. Commodore Dallas, scion of a noted American family, had joined the navy in 1805, fought Barbary pirates, served in the War of 1812 and the Seminole Wars in Florida, and was the commandant of the Pensacola Navy Yard.

Commodore Jones, the oldest member of the tribunal at age seventy-four, was a former doctor who joined the navy at the late age of thirty-one after the death of his wife. One of the officers taken prisoner when USS *Philadelphia* was captured at Tripoli, he fought in the War of 1812 and against Barbary pirates, and held senior commands in the Mediterranean and Pacific. At the time of the tribunal, he was the senior naval officer in New York. Mackenzie's inquiry was a military tribunal and as such was very much in the hands of an older, venerated naval establishment. Hoffman, a forty-nine-year-old former naval midshipman and himself a veteran of the War of 1812, was a lawyer aligned with the Whigs and favored by John Canfield Spencer, a former U.S. congressman and now a U.S. attorney. His job as judge advocate at the court of inquiry was essentially that of a prosecutor, but his role and actions were curtailed by the naval system. He would not be able to aggressively challenge Mackenzie, his officers and crew, or their narratives. The court's hearings lasted for nearly three weeks; among those who stood at the table to testify were Mackenzie's officers, petty officers, and a large number of apprentices and seamen; also testifying were the naval officers who had overseen *Somers'* construction. The first witness was Wales, followed by Gansevoort, part of Mackenzie's strategy of using the witnesses to relay a story that matched his narrative by having the testimony open with a progression that at first matched how the crisis had dawned for Mackenzie and his officers.

What legally minded observers would note was the *ex parte* nature of the proceedings—a one-sided look at Mackenzie and his officers—and with that, an inherent conflict of interest. Mackenzie had asked for and retained command of *Somers*. Every witness from the crew called still served under Mackenzie, and stood before him, across the table, mindful that he still held the power of life and death—or for the officers, thoughts of good references and promotion. In his report to Secretary Upshur, Mackenzie had already recommended promotions, something that John Canfield Spencer had questioned as prejudicial to their testimony. The testimonies given to the Court of Inquiry did not depart from Mackenzie's narrative, and the crew accounts, even those of two of the twelve still under arrest, also fit the larger narrative. There was then and later questions of how much coaching or discussion was held on *Somers* each day as witnesses waited to be called, as *Somers* remained at anchor, near *North Carolina*, the crew retained and under the same officers they had served on during the cruise.

There were some unpleasant surprises for Mackenzie. When he sought to introduce witnesses who would speak to the character of the executed, that was denied. The question of introducing some of Spencer's personal letters into evidence—letters from family, including his mother—was also rejected, and when reported in the papers, this aspect of his defense led to strong denunciations from those who felt that this was going too far. The issue at hand was whether his actions were justified within the limits of reasonable doubt. But the most damning revelation came from a confidential investigation into the conditions of service on board *Somers* ordered by the secretary of the navy as the inquiry started. Evidence from that investigation leaked to the press during the inquiry on January 12.

The leak shared the log book of *Somers* and its entries documenting discipline, and specifically flogging. The picture it painted was horrific; repeated floggings of some, the imposition of multiple lashes on boys, and in all, over 2,200 blows with knotted cord or rope on backs and backsides in the range of six months' time. The summary of the log, published in the New York *Standard* and then shared in other papers, shocked many in the public, even those who might have approved flogging an older seaman for offenses. The record also appalled naval men, including Captain Francis Gregory, commanding officer of USS *North Carolina*. *North Carolina* was one of the navy's receiving and school ships, as will be recalled. As a fellow captain and schoolmaster, Gregory had a strong negative reaction to the imposition of discipline on *Somers* under Mackenzie's command. Gregory was neither a *naif* nor a stranger to the vagaries of command at sea. A veteran with thirty-four years of distinguished service, including a number of actions against the British in the War of 1812, he had warred against pirates in the Gulf and West Indies, and had commanded a number of naval vessels large and small. After *Somers'* arrival, Gregory had gone on board; he later reported to the secretary of the navy that he had not before seen "the crew of an American man-of-war so dirty and dejected in their personal appearances." Many of the men were sick and yet kept at work, trapped on *Somers* other than the thirteen transferred ashore to the Navy Yard's hospital. Gregory also had the twelve "mutineers" taken on board *North Carolina*, and once there had removed heavy manacles and chains as he quickly determined these were not needed.[14]

Gregory took his concerns directly to the secretary. Upshur ordered Commodore Jones to conduct the confidential investigation, and the commodore assigned the task to Captain Gregory. His report, completed and submitted on January 7, as the inquiry continued, sharply criticized the discipline, which had been imposed "with a severity unusual in the service, particularly as regards duty and punishments." In Gregory's opinion—and as the commander of USS *North Carolina* and its hundreds of apprentices, he was a creditable judge—*Somers'* crew was "young, inexperienced . . . unused to the privations of a sea-life, and physically incompetent to perform the duties required on board such a vessel"; an observation that Samuel Cromwell might well have answered with an emphatic yes. *Somers* was a training ship, but the boys packed onto it were too inexperienced. These circumstances, Gregory wrote, "could not fail to break down their spirits; and injure their health." The boys and crew of *Somers* needed to be taken off the brig. While the report remained confidential, the publication of the punishment log in the press infuriated Mackenzie and his supporters and delighted his foes; here again, in pen and ink, was more direct evidence damning Mackenzie's command. The same day, Margaret Cromwell, Samuel's widow, quietly supported by John Canfield Spencer's friends, who likely were acting on the secretary's behalf, appeared before the U.S. District Court and applied for a warrant for the arrest of Mackenzie and Gansevoort for "willful murder." Judge Samuel R. Betts reviewed the application and denied it with a lengthy opinion; it was questionable if he had jurisdiction, as Mackenzie's actions fell under naval law, and the "officers were currently in the midst of a full and searching investigation of their conduct," and were "under competent authority of the President of the United States to be brought to answer before the proper tribunal for any violation of law committed by them, in this most solemn and melancholy transaction."[15]

This alarmed Mackenzie and his supporters; even if the Court of Inquiry ruled that his actions were in accord with naval law, there was the possibility of civil action and lawsuits. A court of inquiry was not the same as a court-martial, and this was what was needed. The Court of Inquiry concluded on January 19, after sitting for nineteen exhausting days. Jones and Stewart commended Mackenzie and his actions, which were "demanded by duty and justified by necessity." Dallas was "disapproving of Mackenzie's conduct."[16] The majority prevailed, and so for the record, the Court of Inquiry ended in Mackenzie's favor. Two days later, the tribunal transmitted their report to Washington for review. By that time, the inquiry's ruling was of no legal consequence, as at Mackenzie's request, the navy had decided on a court-martial. This "will of course terminate the proceedings in this case, as all interference by the civil authority will be unconstitutional, even if the Civil Courts had jurisdiction in the matter."[17] There was a sense of vindication for those who saw Mackenzie a murderer when the navy proceeded with the court-martial. Mackenzie faced five charges that if proved would lead to *his* execution. As charged, Mackenzie had willfully, deliberately, and with malice aforethought hanged Spencer, Cromwell, and Small; oppressed them; and the hangings were illegal punishment in excess of his authority. His conduct had been unbecoming an officer, and that the "mutiny," if there had been discontent, was because he "did oppressively and cruelly use and maltreat the crew."

Four days later, an editorial in the *Tribune* called out for naval reform. "We trust recent occurrences have aided to arouse the public mind to the necessity of a Radical Reform in our navy—a Reform which shall strip that arm of the Public Service of some of its revoltingly aristocratic features. . . . Now it stands out in glaring contrast to every republican maxim—to every idea of Human Equality or Human Rights."[18] With that type of sentiment out in the public, and read by prominent citizens, the navy had to move quickly and decisively. Organizing the court-martial, nonetheless, was difficult, "as almost every officer of the navy has made up his opinion on the subject. One Commodore, who was named as a member, sent out word that if he tried Mackenzie he would bring him in guilty of murder and recommend that he be hanged forthwith."[19]

The court-martial, with orders to assemble on USS *North Carolina* on February 2, 1843, put Mackenzie on trial before a jury of thirteen naval officers. Mackenzie was on trial now not before a jury of his peers, but his superiors. Presiding over the court was

Commodore John Downes, another veteran with decades of distinguished service at sea. The jury of twelve comprised Commodore George C. Read; Captains George Bolton, John Gwinn, John D. Sloat, Daniel Turner, Benjamin Page, Thomas W. Wayman, Joseph Smith, George W. Storer, and Isaac McKeever; and Commanders Henry W. Ogden and Irvine Shubrick. Some were likely more favorable to Mackenzie, others less so; time and the trial would reveal the tenor of the court. Read, another veteran with decades of experience, had served on "Old Ironsides," fought on the ship during the War of 1812, and later commanded *Constitution* among other distinguished assignments. At the time of the trial, Commodore Read was the commandant of the Philadelphia Naval School. Gwinn, a harsh disciplinarian, had served since the War of 1812, and would after the trial assume command of USS *Constitution*, where he gained a harsh reputation for daily floggings of the crew. Sloat, another veteran of long service, was another War of 1812 naval hero, when he had been promoted for gallantry in action. Sloat later commanded the schooner *Grampus*, and in it had fought an action in 1825 against the pirate sloop *Anne*, which ended the career of Puerto Rican pirate Roberto Cofresi. At the time of the trial, Sloat was commandant of the Portsmouth Naval Yard, but within a year would be placed in command of the navy's Pacific Squadron.

Daniel Turner had also fought in the War of 1812, and was close friend of Oliver Hazard Perry, having fought with Perry at the Battle of Lake Erie and subsequently served with him in the Mediterranean and against West Indies pirates; at the time of the trial, he had just returned from a Pacific tour of duty in command of USS *Constitution*. Joseph Smith, a veteran of the War of 1812, had fought with distinction in the Battle of Lake Champlain, commanded the ship-of-the-line USS *Ohio*, and would command the navy's Mediterranean Squadron after the court-martial. George Washington Storer, another decades-serving officer with War of 1812, anti-piracy, Mediterranean, and South American experience, had commanded USS *Potomac* off Brazil when Philip Spencer had failed to distinguish himself in the squadron. He had just returned to the United States and would assume command of the Portsmouth Navy Yard following the court-martial. Isaac McKeever was a War of 1812 veteran whose hard-fought battle against British gunboats off New Orleans in December 1814 ended in defeat, with McKeever wounded, but he and his badly mauled gunboat were the last to surrender in the face of overwhelming odds. He later fought pirates in the West Indies, including a joint mission with British forces to take out Cuban pirates in 1825. Highly esteemed, McKeever had been promoted to captain in 1838, and after the court-martial, would take command of the Brooklyn Navy Yard. Henry W. Ogden, who joined the navy in 1814 and quickly rose to lieutenant, was a trusted officer who most recently had commanded the sloop-of-war USS *Decatur*. His rank of commander and not captain was the result of limits on the number of officers in grade, and it would not be until 1848, and the death of Commodore Charles Ridgely, that he would be advanced in rank.

Irvine Shubrick was the brother of Commodore William Shubrick, and one of James Fenimore Cooper's closest friends. Married into the prominent Du Pont family, Irvine Shubrick was a veteran of the War of 1812 and had served with distinction in the West Indies and the Pacific. Highly regarded, he had been promoted to commander in late 1841, and after the trial would be given command of the sloop-of-war USS *Saratoga*, which was to serve as Commodore Perry's flagship on the African Squadron. Facing the court and Mackenzie was a new judge advocate, William H. Norris, a young attorney from Baltimore and, as the trial proceeded, no fan of Mackenzie. In addition to cross-examination, observers noticed that Norris in the course of the trial assumed more of the role of a "prosecuting attorney, as eager to cast suspicion on Mackenzie's behavior as Mackenzie was to defend it."[20] Mackenzie was also represented by a prominent and successful lawyer, George Griffin. Griffin was a reformer, active in theological and literary circles, and a skilled orator who often commanded a courtroom with his rhetoric and theatrics. Griffin's firm had also handled maritime cases. He was the type of man who would appeal to Mackenzie. Hiring Griffin was at last a wise move by Mackenzie, who had harmed his own defense throughout the inquiry.

The trial proceeded with much of the same testimony, but this time with more cross-examination by the judge advocate, and once more with every day in court avidly followed in the national press. It was also a "must do" for those interested in seeing the trial for themselves, a point of pride to sit in on a celebrated proceeding where a naval officer stood trial before his peers with the possibility of losing his own life at the end. The ship grew so crowded with spectators that the navy shifted the proceedings to the chapel of the Navy Yard. Among the spectators was Philip Hone, who on February 25, 1843, wrote after attending the trial that "the court-martial . . . drags along its tedious length so slowly, and there is such an ever-lasting sameness in the examination, that the public here seems to have lost interest in the matter." Nonetheless, even as public interest was waning, Hone remained interested and hoped for Mackenzie's acquittal despite being disquieted by discrepancies and holes in the defense as Mackenzie was pressed by Norris. "I sometimes think I would like to have evidence of some clearly overt act of mutiny; but I do most entirely believe that he proceeded in his extremity with good motives, in a full conviction." Hone fretted in his diary about the British press making much of the trial, condemning Mackenzie as a "murderer," "coward," "fool," and "bully," leaving "the character of an honoured American officer . . . to be worried and mangled by as filthy a cur as ever barked in foreign accents."[21]

After a nearly two-month-long trial, the court-martial jury drew to a close with the reading of an extensive defense by George Griffin. Hone attended with his daughters and others in the crowded chapel as Griffin read the defense for ninety minutes and listened with delight. Angry at Norris, whose "every artifice . . . to procrastinate the proceedings, exhaust the patience of the court, and worry out the accused and his counsel," Hone praised Griffin's "straightforward appeal to the judgement and patriotism of the court," and closing his argument with a "thrilling and graphic picture" which asked the court to consider what might have happened if "the execution had not taken place; that the unconfined malcontents had risen and released the prisoners; that the mutiny had triumphed, and the brig turned into a piratical cruiser; that the faithful officers and members of the crew had been massacred," sparing Mackenzie to make his way home, to be angrily confronted by the press for what then would follow when "cruising off our coast . . . in an evil hour" Spencer had captured an American ship "plying between this port and Europe, freighted with the talent and beauty of the land":

> The men are all murdered, and the females, including perhaps the new-made wife, and maidens just blooming into woman hood, are forced to become the *brides of pirates*. A universal shriek of agony bursts from the American people throughout their vast domains, and the wailing is echoed back from the whole civilized world; and where then could the commander of the "Somers" have hidden his head, branded as it would have been by a mark of infamy as that illegible as that stamped on the forehead of Cain?[22]

Legal theater is also nothing novel to twentieth- and twenty-first-century court proceedings.

In secret, on March 28, the court voted nine to three that the charges were "not proven," and that they would therefore "acquit Commander Alexander Slidell Mackenzie of the charges and specifications preferred against him by the Secretary of the Navy":[23]

> As these charges involved the life of the accused, and as the finding is in his favor, he is entitled to the benefit of it, as in the analogous case of a verdict of not guilty before a Civil Court, and there is no such power which can constitutionally deprive him of that benefit—The finding, therefore, is simply confirmed and carried into effect without any expression of approbation on the part of the President—no such expression being necessary.

Hone was ecstatic, writing in his diary that the character of the navy had been sustained and "the majesty of the laws vindicated by the full and honorable acquittal." But he worried; "it remains now to be seen whether the vindictive feelings of his enemies can find further means of annoyance and persecution."[24]

Less covered by the press, but still noted, were the subsequent adventures of the twelve men and boys arrested and chained on Mackenzie's orders. The navy did not pursue charges against any of them. Three were from middle-class families whose fortunes had suffered with the Panic of 1837 and its economic aftereffects. That meant that they had the means to fight back for their sons. One of them, George W. Warner, had been enlisted as a boy to serve only until he turned eighteen. When he reached that age on February 5, 1843, his father petitioned the civil courts to have his son released, and on February 9, Warner was released with "no specific charge for mutiny," and "the connection between him and the navy had ceased."[25] The other apprentices and some of the seamen also went to court with legal support to apply for release through the doctrine of habeas corpus. When Mackenzie had learned that Captain Gregory had taken the irons off the prisoners and that they were not confined on *North Carolina*, he had written, still their captain, demanding that they be returned to irons and taken off the ship and lodged in the Navy Yard's prison. One of them, apprentice Eugene Sullivan, had gone to court and the judge, after reviewing the evidence, ordered Sullivan released from imprisonment, though not from the navy, as he had legally enlisted and his term was not up.

That was not the end of Sullivan's woes at the hands of a vindictive Mackenzie. A lengthier legal procedure for him followed in early March because his mother brought suit to compel her son's release. The Sullivans had learned that after his initial civil court ruling, Eugene had been taken to the ship USS *Fulton* at the Navy Yard and again placed in irons and imprisoned. The judge ultimately ruled that he regretted he could not order Sullivan's discharge from the navy "in consequence of improper treatment, because that

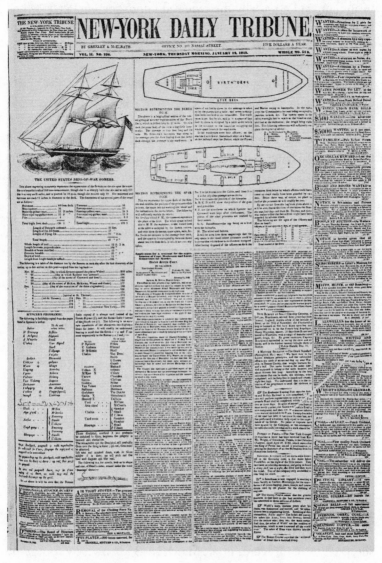

FIGURE 6.1 New York *Tribune* coverage and illustration of *Somers*

treatment, and especially the renewed imprisonment, after he had been discharged by the legal authority, was of such a character as to entitle him a discharge on a proper application to those having the power to annul the contract."[26]

Eight of the "mutineers" appeared in civil court on the morning of February 23 as Mackenzie's own trial continued. After hearing their testimony, the court ordered McKinley and Gallia released, McKinley because he had enlisted without parental permission and Gallia as a foreigner, but that while the "plea for the discharge of the remainder is maltreatment," more time was needed to render judgment in their cases. Ultimately, the court ruled that they should not be kept imprisoned, but they were remanded back to the navy as their terms had not expired. Rather than being pursued by his own enemies, Mackenzie was the one pursuing "further means of annoyance and persecution." His far reach would soon end, as after the court-martial, he was removed as commander of *Somers*, and conditions improved for those ostensible "mutineers" who remained in the navy. In a private letter to Richard Henry Dana Jr., William Watson, assistant to Ogden Hoffman, who had argued against release in court, said that in spite of having by law as the representative of the United States to oppose writs of habeas corpus for the boys, "I do not believe a soul of them had any hand in it. . . . I say to you in confidence that they [the navy] are very willing to let the boys go—the opposition, by instructions, not being very strong."[27]

Meanwhile, Mackenzie's woes were not over; pressure to find civil fault continued, and Mackenzie, not content to let things be, also pursued litigation over libel. While he was able to address some statements that were mistakes of fact, his own legal fights to continue to define the narrative of what had happened were not always rousing successes. A victory came in late March 1843 when a New York grand jury, under pressure to indict Mackenzie, voted twelve to eleven to not take up the challenge after Ogden Hoffman appeared and persuasively argued against it on constitutional grounds. Less satisfactory was another case instituted by Mackenzie. Under pressure on

the witness stand in a libel suit filed by Mackenzie against the pub-
lisher of the New York *Journal of Commerce*, which had published in
its account of the verdict that "seven out of the twelve were of opinion that the charges or some of them, had been proved," Captain
Isaac McKeever, as a member of the court-martial, while not naming
who voted, testified that on the three charges against Mackenzie, the
court-martial's officers noted nine to three to acquit. The votes were
all "viva voce" and audibly pronounced in the privacy of their delib-
erations, so he heard them clearly.[28] They were:

> On the first charge of Murder on Board a United States Vessel
>   on the High Sea, "proved in the second degree," or murder
>   with malice;
> On the second charge of Oppression, "proved";
> On the third charge of Illegal Punishment, "proved."

Another Mackenzie legal tangle was an action where he was again
the defendant. Charles Wilson, one of the twelve now released,
never formally charged "mutineers," sued Mackenzie in Brooklyn.[29]

Wilson's lawyer, John B. Scoles, a prominent local attorney
and former Whig state assemblyman, asked for damages. The suit
against Mackenzie claimed damages for Wilson's suffering. After his
arrest, he was "kept on deck, double ironed and exposed in midwin-
ter . . . his feet were frozen, and he has been from that time to the
present, afflicted with rheumatism." Instead of a trial once *Somers*
reached New York, he and the others were never charged or tried,
but kept imprisoned until he and the others had successfully sought
relief through habeas corpus. Mackenzie's lawyers fought back, argu-
ing again that Mackenzie could not be tried in civil courts for his
actions as a naval officer. The judge agreed, and the case went on
appeal to the State Supreme Court. The Supreme Court ruled that an
action "may be maintained against an officer of the navy for illegally
assaulting and imprisoning one of his subordinates, though the act
was done upon the high seas, and under color of navy discipline." By

asserting the legal right of Wilson to sue Mackenzie, Scoles had been proven right; for the first time since 1843, Mackenzie once again faced potential peril in local and state courts. The fight picked up again when the trial was sent back to the local court to be retried in April 1846. That case was set back when Mackenzie's lawyers argued that the suit should have been brought for malicious prosecution, or a wanton exercise of Mackenzie's authority. The judge should dismiss the case, which he did. While a victory of sorts, the fight with his former crewmember kept Mackenzie's name in the press, reinforced a negative view of him among those who had already decided they did not like the captain, and continued to take time and money and bring unrelenting wear to Mackenzie, his family, and his friends.

What also followed were three powerful contemporary non-court "indictments" of Mackenzie using trial by pamphlet. The first was his old nemesis James Fenimore Cooper, whose enmity stemmed from Mackenzie's attack on his *History of the Navy* on behalf of aggrieved Perry clan members who felt Oliver Hazard's role in the Battle of Lake Erie had somehow been slighted by Cooper. Never one to take an insult lightly, Cooper grappled with Mackenzie in writing, and the verbal broadsides were often brutal. Now, with Mackenzie acquitted but not universally embraced, Cooper struck in a measured, delayed response. In his attack, Cooper was aided by secret correspondence with the judge advocate, William H. Norris, himself no fan of Mackenzie's. Norris "fed Cooper pages and pages of secret 'memoranda' which condemn Mackenzie as a diabolical fraud and point to specific contradictions in his testimony." Cooper used the intelligence, but "recognizing its shrillness, toned it down to a clinical examination of the facts."[30] Nonetheless, it was exceptionally damaging to Mackenzie.

Norris' basic premise was that Gansevoort, "a nervous, blundering fellow, who rather than be still, would cut from a tree the limb which held him up," when told of the conversation by Wales, went "wild with suspicion, and ultimately, got Mackenzie to see that a 'mutiny must be believed in now,'" and agreed to a "clear case of fraud, management and virtual conspiracy." Norris also believed

FIGURE 6.2 James Fenimore Cooper

that Mackenzie had manufactured the supposed conversation, part confession from Spencer that he presented at the trial, but only after asking for a few days off because he was ill. The suspicion was that Mackenzie had "taken ill" to retreat home and write it when the court had demanded it, and he had offered to retrieve it. Cooper's cool dissection of Mackenzie's case would become even more apparent in the decades to come.

Another exceptionally harmful blow to Mackenzie was a three-part article written by William Sturgis (1782–1863). Captain Sturgis was a prominent mariner, wealthy Boston merchant, and a politician. His extensive and notable career as a seagoing leader in the Pacific's nascent maritime fur trade and the China trade gave him powerful credibility. Sturgis' account was devastating. It would continue to resonate years later. At home, surrounded by friends and admirers, Mackenzie found some respite in the midst of that adoration and other expressions of support, but he also tried to salve his wounds after reading Cooper's pamphlet, which he decried as "sophistry and venomous abuse," with a lengthy response in the fifth edition of his republished life of Oliver Hazard Perry, returning to the source of his initial dispute with Cooper.

Reading both, the conclusion of many remained the same; Mackenzie's focus was more ad hominem, never a strong point in debate, while Cooper, not disdaining the ad hominem, made some very good legal and seafaring points, as did Sturgis' article and another damning anonymous pamphlet. Mackenzie's friends and fans rallied for him, including Dana and a young Boston attorney, soon to achieve national prominence and ultimate election to the U.S. Senate, Charles Sumner. Sumner defended Mackenzie fiercely and brilliantly in a July 1843 article, noting that a key principle of the law stated that "a person having judicial authority will be protected by the law in all cases where he exercised it honestly and conscientiously, even though grievous error may have occurred."[31] The arguments continued through the year and beyond, passing from court of inquiry and court-martial, as scholar Harrison Hayford noted, into the court of opinion. There it would remain, with additional information coming available, as well as more muddying of the waters, a story that timelessly would return to the headlines as the decades passed, turned into centuries, and *Somers* and the *Somers* Affair passed from living memory, but never from the public's fascination.

Chapter 7

"Damn Bad Luck Follows"

With the end of the court-martial and Mackenzie's acquittal, any thoughts that the storm had passed were shaken the next day. That night, on Friday, March 31, 1843, *Somers'* surgeon Richard Leecock walked past Purser Heiskell, who sat at the table in the wardroom working on his accounts. Leecock said nothing, stopped at the end of the small compartment, stood by the drawers where the officers stowed clothes, turned back toward Heiskell, and put a pistol up to his forehead then shot himself above the right eye. He remained standing, not yet dead, but the heavy lead ball had punched through his skull and into his brain. Leecock slowly leaned back, still upright, but sagging against the drawers.[1] Heiskell and another crewman rushed over and lowered him to the deck, where "he immediately expired." "The sad occurrence," noted the papers, "is attributed to a settled melancholy and partial derangement induced by a long and severe attack of the yellow fever."[2]

Somers was a bad-luck ship, and quietly around the waterfront and in naval ranks word spread that the brig was cursed. Regardless of personal belief in curses, the events of the cruise of the brig *Somers* followed both the ship and the lives of many of those associated with it to bad effect. Was there a "mutiny"? Were there "mutineers"? Was Spencer innocent, and Mackenzie guilty, or was the opposite true? There was then, and there remains to this day, no clear definition of who was right and who was wrong; what seems clear in twenty-first-century hindsight is that all parties shared in the blame; Mackenzie and Spencer were a volatile combination on a crowded, small vessel too difficult to handle both physically as a craft and as a focus of training and discipline. Social historian Kristopher Mecholsky asserts that the saga of *Somers* is a powerful example of an American true-crime narrative.[3] There is no single story. There were and are multiple narratives, some sensational, untrue, and some deliberately slanted in terms of the writer's bias toward one side or the other. Dominating the news, the *Somers* Affair was the harbinger of late twentieth- and early twenty-first-century modern crime stories that play out on network television and social media. Pundits opine at one end of the spectrum or the other, and what gets lost is what rests in the middle. And the story of the *Somers* "mutiny" is a tale in which there is no hero.

The *Somers* affair effectively ruined the lives of many of those who played a role in it. It held up a mirror to an ugly aspect of society, the consequences of different rules for the sons of the prominent or rich; Philip Spencer's transgressions were excused and he was shifted from ship to ship until he finally reached the deck of *Somers*. Mackenzie embodies the American dream; his family had risen from working-class circumstances and he had become not only an officer and a gentleman, but through marriage, was also associated with an American naval "aristocratic" family. And yet his origins, like those of his brother, were not forgotten by a New York upper-crust society that could put down his brother with a barbed comment that reflects his father's honest, hard work in a soap and candle factory; he, too, had been "dipped," not "molded" in society. Then Mackenzie found himself with, as he said, the base son of an honorable father, a lad who could seemingly do no wrong in the eyes of his superiors, who feared John Canfield Spencer. Despite what would be inferred years later, there was no innocence to Philip Spencer. Philip Spencer was *not* Billy Budd. "Billy Budd is the personification of goodness and innocence," well-liked if not loved by his peers, guileless and moral.[4]

Mackenzie, surrounded by the sons and nephews of the Perry clan, had an incredible weight put on his shoulders in his first command. There were also whatever internal voices were in his head about his family, and his own hard rise to limited fame, to being a good travel writer, but not the next Longfellow or Cooper. He was in his forties at last a commander after a very long time as a junior officer. Now came a cruise with a young man he likely saw as squandering his familial advantages. Spencer sneered behind his back, mocked him just out of earshot, and acted as if there were no consequences. The reality was that when the consequences came, they were too severe, too quick, and yet the consequences fell not solely on Spencer. Mackenzie, a man who loved words, said too much. "Oh, that mine enemy should write such a book," delightedly noted his foes.[5]

They used those words to pillory Mackenzie, who was "tried and convicted" in the eyes of a number of his fellow citizens in the court of public opinion. But public opinion was split, and there were many testimonials to Mackenzie's character and judgment, friends raising funds to pay his costs during the long inquiry, court-martial, and a subsequent lawsuit. As diarist Philip Hone noted, there were friends who "lament the necessity, while they justify the motives, of the dreadful act of discipline which was called upon to perform."[6] Richard Henry Dana Jr., writing Mackenzie privately, noted that the sentiment he heard, from "the educated people, in the professions, and in what we call in America the upper classes, you were . . . a hero, and not a hero of the sword, but the hero of a moral conflict."[7]

And yet, the reality of the dream is that American values were upheld; Mackenzie was not hanged although he had slain the son of an American lord. The court-martial absolved him—but not unanimously. He was damaged, and he remained ashore until he briefly again commanded a ship in the U.S. Navy years later. But whether that was unspoken punishment or his own withdrawal from the public eye was not enough for his critics. Mackenzie's acquittal did not go over well with John Canfield Spencer. At the next cabinet meeting after the verdict and Mackenzie's acquittal, Spencer angrily confronted Upshur. The dispute quickly turned into a fistfight, with Upshur breaking a stool or a chair over Spencer's head. President Tyler broke up the fight.

This highlighted a certain reality known to some at the time. But for circumstance, a young, angry, and easy-to-fight John Canfield Spencer might have faced a different life had he not been the son of Ambrose Spencer, with his wilder impulses tamed in youth.

Things were never quite right after that with either Upshur or the president; John Canfield Spencer, in a public speech in 1851, referred to Tyler as a "weak and wayward President," and Tyler would comment privately that when the court-martial rendered its verdict and acquitted Mackenzie, "I could do nothing but approve the sentence. If it had ordered Mackenzie to be shot, I would not interposed to save him. Spencer, then still Secretary of War, was very urgent with me to set aside the trial, & to order another for the slayer of his son."[8] Tyler pointedly reminded his secretary of war of the rule of law and that in America, double jeopardy did not apply, especially when Mackenzie had been fairly tried.

The nature of the Spencer men bears some examination. John Canfield Spencer was eulogized by one who knew him as "a man in whom intellect and sterner features prevailed and stamped the character." Spencer was admired, but not liked; the execution of Philip brought sympathy, but primarily for Mrs. Spencer. However, a Spencer contemporary noted that John Canfield Spencer's "clear voice and decided attitude . . . command our admiration." That is, unless you are his child and at the table of a father who "expressed himself in words of burning sarcasm," one aspect of a character that embodied both "a cold nature" and yet a "mild, and somewhat courtly . . . winning gentleness and candor." As to their relationship with their mother, less is known, other than the sad but telling comment from Philip that news of his execution would kill her. It did not, but she went into protracted mourning. His father flew into a cold rage. There is no known surviving record of what Philip's siblings thought, but there is a possibility, if there was any self-reflection, that the thought might have been, "There but for the grace of God go I."

Philip's older brothers John Canfield Spencer Jr. and Ambrose Spencer were troubled and troublesome. Both of them were accused of forging their father's name to cover bills and cash checks, a crime Philip also confessed to his father. After the trials, a visitor to Mackenzie's home, after discussing the events on the brig, was allowed to see a collection of papers that included the personal letters Philip Spencer had on board *Somers* that the captain had confiscated. After reading them, he wrote to his wife that "A greater deeper dyed scamp probably never lived. He robbed his father repeatedly, as a brother of his forged the father's name and was actually already to be put on trial."[9] That brother was John Canfield Spencer Jr., who upon graduating from Hobart College in 1842 was shipped off to sea after forging checks in his father's name. In very short order he joined the navy through the good offices of his uncle, William Augustus Spencer. Appointed to the rank of captain in early 1841, Uncle William had escorted Philip to USS *North Carolina*, and took John Jr. to sea with him as captain's clerk on USS *Columbia*, his own command.

They were at sea when Philip was hanged, but when *Columbia* reached the port of Genoa, Italy, the news reached the ship. One of the officers, William Parker, recalled late in life that the news "caused much excitement on board our ship, as our captain was the uncle of Midshipman Spencer, and the captain's clerk was his brother."[10] Parker noted, as was the unspoken practice among the officer corps at the time, that while different opinions "have been held as the action of Captain Mackenzie," "I do not propose to discuss it." John Canfield Spencer Jr. apparently adjusted his course in life, and was promoted to purser in August 1843, but like Philip, he also died at sea. While serving in the African Squadron, patrolling off the coast of Dahomey, he died of "fever" on December 29, 1845, and was buried under the walls of the fort at the port of Ouidah. His uncle, William A., died just after the one-year anniversary of his nephew's execution on *Somers*. Sixty years later, a reminiscence of the navy at that time suggested that Philip's execution had led to Captain Spencer resigning his commission, but in the view of the officer whose reminiscences noted the event, Captain Spencer's departure was no loss as he had "ruined" the ship he commanded through "incapacity and stubbornness" and rages like one where "he stamped the deck, pulled his hair, and made use of hearty expressions not found in prayer books" when *Columbia* was at Genoa.[11]

The longer life and career of the oldest Spencer son, Ambrose, shows an even stronger tie to the personality disorder that had to have afflicted Philip. Ambrose attended Middlebury College in Vermont after graduating from the Canandaigua Academy, but failed to graduate from it. He married a local woman and they moved to Cleveland, where he became a lawyer. When the news of Philip's execution reached the press and quickly became a national story, stories emerged, whether true or not, that Ambrose had been arrested in Albany and charged with forging his father's name for bills due to a broker and to a hotel proprietor. The Bangor *Daily Whig and Courier* first relayed the news in February 1842 that this "strange, inconsistent and foolish conduct" of Ambrose's was so uncharacteristic that "his afflicted family are confident he must be laboring under an alienation of mind."[12] This allusion to mental illness in the family was not a clinical diagnosis, but rather a defense that perhaps he had become temporarily insane. That case was brought up again with fervor following Philip's death. If there was any "alienation of mind," it was not confined to Ambrose.

The Bangor *Daily Whig and Courier* of August 10, 1843, in rehashing the old news, also noted that "young Spencer, the son of John C. Spencer, who committed various forgeries and ran away to Texas is among the gang of pseudo-Texan banditti under Col. Snively, which is prowling along our Western border to plunder Santa Fe traders," while another account had Ambrose at sea as a pirate in the Gulf of Mexico. The truth was that Ambrose Spencer was in Texas, acting as judge advocate for a group of Republic of Texas mercenaries led by Jacob Snively, who had set out to attack and plunder a Mexican wagon train on the Santa Fe Trail in retaliation for Mexican raids on the newly independent Republic and Mexico's seizure of a Texas wagon train on the trail. When the Texans crossed into U.S. territory in late June 1843, it led to an international incident. They were stopped by U.S. dragoons who were guarding the frontier and escorting the Mexicans as they transited through to Santa Fe. After a tense standoff, the dragoons ultimately disarmed the Texans, whom they called "land pirates," and escorted some to Independence, Missouri, and left the others to ultimately break into smaller groups and return home.[13] It had to be an embarrassment for the former secretary of war, now secretary of the treasury as of March 1843, to have another son in the news running awry of U.S. military justice, although Ambrose did not get hanged.

Ambrose Spencer returned home to his wife and children, and moved with them all to the South, where he and his wife Agnes served as both teachers and principals of academies in Gwinnett County, Georgia, and Darlington, South Carolina. Spencer was not popular, with a reputation for being "high-tempered," challenging a local man to a duel and shooting at another. He lied about being a graduate of West Point, and showed off scars from "a wild life on the frontier." There had to be other problems, too, at home, because by 1850 Agnes left South Carolina and returned to Middlebury without him. When John Canfield Spencer died in 1854, he left nothing in his will to Ambrose, whom he only acknowledged as "A. Spencer," and not as his son. He did, however, take care to ensure that Agnes and the children had a one-third stake in his estate. Ambrose remained in the South, moving to Georgia and settling in Savannah to practice as a lawyer, where Agnes and the children rejoined him. When the Civil War broke out, he served as a Confederate soldier, never advancing beyond the rank of corporal. That did not stop him, postwar, from assuming the title of "Colonel Spencer." By 1864, he had settled near Andersonville, where the Confederacy kept a military prison camp crowded with more than 45,000 prisoners of war in desperate conditions penned inside a wooden stockade.

The crowding and unsanitary conditions killed some 13,000 of the men held at Andersonville through malnutrition, disease, and exposure. Spencer claimed that he and Agnes had entered the camp to provide aid and comfort for the prisoners, and that he secretly been working for the Union cause. When the war ended, he emerged from parole as a former Confederate soldier and plunged into the national limelight as a special witness for the U.S. government in the prosecution of Henry Wirz, the Confederate commander of Andersonville, for murder. "Colonel Spencer's" tales of cruelty, deliberate starvation, and murder, even poisoning, were national news, but Wirz's lawyer was no fool, and he discredited Spencer as a liar. That did not stop the government from convicting and hanging Wirz. Despite the shaming he endured in the courtroom, Spencer emerged from the trial nationally famous. He was shameless. His book, *A Narrative of Andersonville* (1866), was a national bestseller, even though it was attacked even by former prisoners as "fallacious." Lies exposed, and deeply unpopular, he and his family fled Georgia in 1867 and moved to Chicago. There, he and Agnes again separated. Back to being a lawyer, despite no degree in law or a license, he moved to Marion, Illinois, where as a lawyer he prosecuted local Klansmen for a murder. He failed to get a conviction, was sued by the defendants for false imprisonment, and was himself imprisoned.[14]

Freed from jail, Spencer moved to Missouri. Agnes did not follow, nor did they divorce, but that did not stop the "Colonel" from marrying Laura Alice Murphy, and "adopting" her son from her marriage to William John Jeffers of Texas. Laura Alice left Jeffers when she found that he was already married before he had married her, but did not get a divorce, which meant in a thoroughly modern messy way, bigamy united the three in a fashion that could only end up badly. The last act in Ambrose Spencer's life played out melodramatically. Although he spent all of his new wife's money, she stayed with him even when Jeffers asked her to return. It all came to a head in April 1876, in Linn, Missouri. Spencer, living with the former Mrs. Jeffers as Mrs. Spencer, was now an insurance agent and lawyer, and a "notable" citizen. William Jeffers came to town, confronted Laura at home, demanding to see Ambrose, and left when he found the "Colonel" was not there. Jeffers found Spencer at a nearby stable, shot at him three times, and missed. Undeterred, he chased Spencer into the street and shot him through the head, leaving a fatal wound with "the brains oozing out both sides." Once again, one of the Spencer boys made the national news, with one eulogist noting he was "a somewhat dissolute man, a man of unusual talent and ability," but nonetheless, a doomed one, like his brother. "We are a believer in Fate . . . some men, and some families, are victims of destiny."[15]

The destiny of others involved in the *Somers* Affair also betray the less beneficent aspect of fate. Abel Upshur shifted from secretary of the navy to secretary of state at President Tyler's request a few months after the trial. Damn bad luck followed him. Loyal to Tyler and still interested in naval reform, Upshur joined the president and other dignitaries on February 26, 1844, on a Potomac River cruise on USS *Princeton*. *Princeton*, a relatively new ship, was steam-powered and fitted with a propeller instead of sidewheels. The ship was an embodiment of what naval reformers and friends had advocated—a shift to more modern vessels with the latest technology to match an improved, more professional naval corps. Technological improvements for warships also included making bigger guns with longer ranges, all part of an early naval arms race. The first stirrings of that naval arms race included not only the construction of USS *Princeton*, but also the creation of an experimental naval gun known as the "Peacemaker"—a massive weapon constructed from wrought iron (guns like this were usually made of cast iron), and like *Princeton*, manufactured during Upshur's time as secretary of the navy. Designed by Swedish American inventor John Ericsson and naval officer Captain Robert F. Stockton, the gun was touted as "the most formidable ordnance ever mounted." It could fire a 212-pound shell over two miles.

The cruise on USS *Princeton* was an opportunity to show off the new ship and the large gun, which had recently been installed on *Princeton*. *Princeton* was crowded with hundreds of dignitaries, including the president, his fiancée, cabinet officials, congressmen and senators, and foreign ministers, in all, a crowd of nearly four

hundred men and women. Captain Stockton, with a gun crew, read-
ied and fired *Peacemaker*—once, twice, and then a third time. The
third time, instead of firing, the gun exploded at its breech, sending chunks of iron into the crowd as a dense cloud of smoke covered the deck. As it cleared, after a "solemn deathlike and dreadfully
awful silence," dozens of bodies lay around the gun. Three of them
had been struck by a large fragment, and "the blood was running in
crimson streams down the deck," with "their countenances so black-
ened by the smoke of the powder and so distorted in the agonies of
death" that initial witnesses could not easily identify them. One of
those men was Abel Upshur, and lying next to him was the newly
appointed secretary of the navy, Thomas Gilmer. In addition to several dead, dozens were mangled, and the deck was covered with severed arms and legs. Legend has it that scattered among the carnage
was Upshur's severed head. The former secretary of the navy, naval
reformer, and advocate of a new, more powerful navy had once again
been caught up in an experiment gone terribly wrong in the quest to
develop a stronger, better U.S. Navy.[16]

Alexander Slidell Mackenzie did not lose his life, but his was for-
ever changed, and not for the better. While he had defenders in addition to his detractors, some of them powerful on both sides of the
question, his naval career was on hold. His legal perils were not over.
Sailmaker's Mate Charles Wilson, one of the men arrested and confined on *Somers*, sued Mackenzie in New York State Supreme Court
for assault and battery and false imprisonment. Mackenzie asked
for the case to be dismissed, but the court ruled that the suit would
continue because "officers of the navy are answerable in damages
for cruel treatment to subordinates, even if it occurs upon the high
seas or in a foreign port," and awarded Wilson damages to be collected from his former captain.[17] Mackenzie's wife later recalled that
the four months of questioning and defense in the court of inquiry
and the court-martial were "scenes of daily trial such as few have
known," yet he had been sustained by expressions of support, but
also acknowledging that he had intensely suffered personally "such

as few could know because few have the capacity so keenly to feel."[18] Returning home to his family "estate," prime acreage overlooking the Hudson River north of Manhattan in Tarrytown, New York, Mackenzie and his family lived in their country farmhouse until the summer of 1846, when he was recalled to duty, but not given a ship.

He spent the time with his wife, Catherine Alexander Robinson Mackenzie, their two sons, three-year-old Ranald and one-year old Alexander Jr., and two daughters born during his shore leave, Harriet and May. The Mackenzies entertained notable guests, and he engrossed himself in "reading, writing and superintending his farm," which was "an occupation in which he took great delight," his wife later reminisced. The writing was a new naval history, the life of early naval hero Stephen Decatur, which he published in 1846. The visitors who called, while admittedly partial enough to come and stay, included people who had never known Mackenzie prior to the cause célèbre. Those guests were surprised by Mackenzie's "manner and personality"; visitor Francis Lieber wrote in August 1843 that "Mackenzie is one of the simplest, unfashionablest, kindest, plainest men I know,"[19] while Richard Henry Dana Jr. described him, after meeting Mackenzie, as "quiet, unassuming, free from all military display in manner, self-possessed, and with every mark of a human, conscientious man, with sound judgement and moral courage."[20] As historian Harrison Hayford noted, "this image of the man" forces us "to reconsider our previous judgements, though not necessarily to change them."[21]

With Texas admitted to the United States and the subsequent war with Mexico, Mackenzie was recalled to service as a secret agent of newly elected president James K. Polk to Cuba; this followed a secret mission by his brother, John Slidell, who had been sent to Mexico with an offer to buy much of Mexico's territories in order to stave off war. When the Mexican government refused Slidell's offer, the president sent Mackenzie to Cuba to recruit former dicta-tor, and villain of the Alamo, General Antonio López de Santa Anna, who was then in exile in Cuba. Santa Anna offered to settle with the

United States if the country allowed him passage to return to Mexico. Once in Mexico, Santa Anna reneged on the deal, and the United States ended up fighting him as Mexico's leader in the Mexican War of 1846–1848. That conflict returned Alexander Slidell Mackenzie to active duty. He was assigned as ordnance officer of the steam frigate USS *Mississippi*, commanded by his brother-in-law Matthew Perry, to join the Mexican War off Veracruz. After a lengthy blockade in which *Somers* and other U.S. ships patrolled the waters off the port, the first major amphibious landing in U.S. military history took place. As part of that endeavor, Mackenzie supervised landing heavy naval guns to batter the city's walls. The guns Mackenzie personally commanded ashore were next to guns manned by the crew of *Somers*. It was not so much irony, more a result of a smaller navy in those days.

Close by at another gun battery was Mackenzie's former clerk from *Somers*, Lieutenant Oliver Hazard Perry Jr., now commanding guns of his own. Veracruz fell after a twenty-day siege. Mackenzie remained with *Mississippi*, taking part in naval excursions and forays and surveying the coast with Perry. Back home in August 1847, he received orders to return to sea and command USS *Mississippi*. Returning to the Gulf and the Mexican War, Mackenzie did not stay long. He sailed home in April 1848, and returned to the farm. The navy granted him a three-month leave. His health was poor, though, and the leave was extended. On September 13, 1848, Mackenzie went out for a horseback ride to the village of Ossining. Once there, as his horse trotted down the street, he was struck by a powerful heart attack, fell off his horse, struck his head on the pavement, and died.[22] He was forty-five years old. Mackenzie was buried in Saint Mark's Church-in-the-Bowery's churchyard, the burial ground of many prominent New Yorkers, a final resting place that Mackenzie would have approved of, and left his widow Catherine with five children ranging in age from six years to five months old, the youngest child, Morris, having been born in May while his father was still at sea. To ensure an income for herself and the children, Catherine

Mackenzie sold the family farm to Edwin Bartlett, cofounder of the Pacific Mail Steamship Company. Bartlett had the farmhouse torn down to build a mansion on the estate.

The fortunes and fates of other *Somers* officers and crew stand out occasionally in the years and then decades that followed the "mutiny." *Somers* itself was frequently mentioned in the news; it now had the status of a tainted celebrity. They always stood out and the brig was mentioned when sordid circumstances or violent ends were the focus of the news. *Somers* also gained a sensational reputation as a "floating gallows," and as a cursed ship. A "poetic infusion" published by the New York *Herald* in May 1843 asserted in its verses that the brig was haunted, and "often on that gallows spar, The yardsmen brave will quail, In the midnight watch at figures three, Unearthly—fleshless—pale" would appear.

Death would come for them all, as the ghosts of the dead men carried *Somers* to its demise:

Better far to yield her then
At once unto the dead,
Than to keep the bloody, cursed craft,
An honest seaman's dread.
Take—take her far away from land,
Her rudder lashed midship:
From every yard-arm, fore and main
Let hang the murderous whip.
Sheet home on every cursed spar,
Set every rag of sail,
And leave her to the ocean ghouls,
And demons of the gale![23]

This is as melodramatic as a mid-nineteenth-century poem can be. It set into many minds, including superstitious sailors, that *Somers* was indeed both haunted and doomed, as were those who had hanged Spencer, Cromwell, and Small.

Robert Rogers, who met Spencer in Rio de Janeiro and offered a lengthy and damning indictment of Spencer's faults, was ultimately destined to serve on *Somers* after the events of the first of December. Late in life, Rogers noted that the whole story was "as pathetic as one could find, but it does not end with Spencer."[24] In addition, "The vessel which he sought to capture, and from whose yard-arm he was hanged, seemed to have been in some indeterminate way incorporated with his destiny; banned and fated by some latent influence which we may deride, but often fear." Rogers recalled his shipmates' reactions when he joined *Somers* three years after the "mutiny." "Get out of that craft as soon as you can, for sooner or later she's bound to go to the devil. Since the mutiny damn bad luck goes with her."[25] And, "Some night you'll see Spencer swinging from the yard-arm from which he was hanged, as he, and the others, have been seen time and again."[26] Rogers remembered those warnings when he looked up on several occasions at night, and while the crew worked to reef the topsails—pulling the loose canvas close to be lashed tightly to the yards—to see "their folds, at times, assume human shapes, which my fancy of fear fashioned to the form of the suspended mutineers."[27]

But as to whether it was his imagination or others, he recalled one night in particular, as the wind howled and the men worked aloft, to look up to see them huddled against the mast, not moving, "sail loose and loudly flapping." He climbed up and confronted them; the "captain of the foretop," the enlisted man in charge of the sailors working, pointed to the yardarm. "I see nothing," Rogers yelled. "Spencer and Small," the man yelled back. "Don't you see them?" Rogers said that fear and imagination "did really for a moment persuade me that I saw Spencer's ghost." The next day, he tried to console the man with the observation that it had all been a trick of the night and imagination. The man answered, "All right, sir, All right. There are things you gentlemen abaft the mainmast don't see, and if you did you wouldn't laugh at them. But mark my words, the brig's doomed. She'll never see port again, and a good many of us will go down with her."[28]

FIGURE 7.1 Sailors furling sails in the top

In 1855, a sensational story in the Boston *Flag of Our Union* reported that every witness at the *Somers* proceedings "has since died a violent death." This was refuted by the Louisville *Courier-Journal's* editor, who, forgetting Mackenzie, noted that while Leecock had died, a number of the officers were doing well, among them Gansevoort, Henry Rodgers, "promoted to lieutenant," Egbert Thompson, "promoted . . . and now in the Mediterranean," Charles W. Hayes, "promoted" and "stationed off Brazil. Purser Heiskell is in the Portsmouth navy-yard. Lieutenant M. C. Perry is in the coast survey. O. H. Perry is secretary of legation to a foreign court. . . . Midshipman Deslonde is residing in Louisiana," and last "our friend James W. Wales, of this city . . . looks as if he has no intention of dying in any way for a long time to come."[29]

A year after the court-martial, in 1844, Purser Wales received a gold medal from "a number of the citizens of Louisville," where he lived. The medal was engraved to Wales to "testify their gratitude and admiration" for his "heroic conduct and fearless fidelity" when "mutiny was about to cause the destruction of the lives of American seamen."[30] Meanwhile, the brig itself received no accolades. Instead, *Somers* was found by inspection to be so badly infested with rats that the navy ordered the brig "dismantled and hauled upon the marine railway" for repairs. "Before she was removed to the railway her hold was filled with steam from the city ice-boat, and kept so for several hours, in order to kill the rats."[31] In October 1845, Philadelphia newspapers reported that Frederick Snyder, "one of the crew of the brig *Somers* at the time of the mutiny," was walking "with a female" and believed that three men following him meant harm. He attacked them with a stick of firewood, and beat one of the men to death. The editor of the *Southport Telegraph* in Wisconsin, reporting on Snyder's arrest, quoted the Racine *Advocate*'s account that noted "Had Capt. McKenzie hung up this man Snyder with the other three mutineers, one human life at least would have been saved."[32]

A definite fatality was the apprentice system for young officers, which continued on the receiving ships in the navy yards for young seamen. In November 1845, national news reports noted that "the practice of recruiting boys into the navy as apprentices was abolished by Secretary Upshur, soon after the murder of young Spencer. The crew of the *Somers*, it will be recollected, was composed of a large majority of apprentices."[33] A more critical and knowledgeable observer, Robert Rogers, noted in his late-life account that the entire system of apprenticing, the harsh conditions of life for seamen in the U.S. Navy in that era, and the influx of non-American recruits, including the boys, from destitute as well as what many saw as sordid circumstances had conspired on *Somers* to give Spencer "good impressible material to practice his deviltry upon."

Rogers, based on his experience, believed that the boys on *Somers* "were reckless, vicious, destitute of all fixed principles of morality and patriotism," given many had been recruited from the streets from homeless, hand-to-mouth circumstances. They were then placed into "an isolated life at sea on board a man-of-war. At best it is a lazy and depraved existence, at least before the mast."[34] That life, Rogers averred, was not conducive to turning out good seamen. "Where one turns out the good apprentice, ten steadily pursue the 'Rakes Progress.'" While perhaps an overstatement, Rogers' observations were shared by senior officials and politicians, and the events on *Somers*, on a ship purposely built for and dispatched to deal with the very problem, hammered home the point of needing a new system. The first move to that new system came when the long-desired plan of naval reformers to create an academy for training officers not unlike that for army officers convinced Navy Secretary George Bancroft to open a naval school at Fort Severn, in Annapolis, Maryland, in October 1845. In 1850, the school was designated as the U.S. Naval Academy.

Meanwhile, after *Somers* had lain at anchor off Brooklyn throughout the trials, it departed to sea with a regular crew, a training brig no more. Assigned to the Home Squadron under the command of Lieutenant John West, *Somers* was quickly dispatched with other warships to the Gulf of Mexico as the entry of Texas into the United States as the twenty-eighth state in December 1845 led to increased tensions with Mexico. The relationship was already strained by American support for the Texas revolution and an unconcealed U.S. desire to acquire Mexican California. Despite the machinations of some, including Alexander Slidell Mackenzie, as noted earlier, to avert it through diplomacy or outright bribery, war broke out in April 1846 after brief skirmishes between American and Mexican forces along the jointly disputed Texas-Mexico border. The first major battle, on the plains of Palo Alto, near modern Brownsville, Texas, was a victory for American General Zachary Taylor, with much heavier casualties on the Mexican side. However, the road to Mexico City and victory was not going to be an easy battle, and the decision to blockade and then take the port of Veracruz, and from there drive into Mexico City, as Hernan Cortés had done three centuries earlier, became the American strategy.

The Navy Department ordered *Somers* to help blockade Veracruz, heavily defended by massive forts and known as the "Gibraltar of the Gulf." That was when Mackenzie landed and helped batter the walls of the fortress of San Juan de Ulua into submission. But by the time those guns started to pound stone and brick into rubble, *Somers* was gone. *Somers'* last days afloat were spent anchored off Veracruz, waiting to catch any ships attempting to run the U.S. Navy's blockade of the port in an attempt to strangle trade. *Somers* was under the command of Lieutenant Raphael Semmes, a thirty-seven-year-old Southerner and a twenty-year veteran of the navy. Semmes had assumed command to replace Commander Duncan Ingraham, a fellow Southerner, who "had worn himself out by incessant toil on the blockade, and was obliged, reluctantly, to return home."[35] Semmes made no comment on the brig's reputation in his memoir of the war other than *Somers* being "a fast and active vessel . . . a very efficient blockader." The initial account of *Somers'* loss noted that the brig's time off Veracruz, "performing the most active blockading duties for several months, exposed to every vicissitude of weather," was about to end in a day or two. On the night of December 7, 1846, Semmes anchored *Somers* off Isla Verde, in the lee of the island to ride safe from the occasional *nortes*, winter squalls that came in from the sea.

The next morning, *Somers'* watch spotted a brig in the distance, making for Veracruz. Semmes ordered all hands to action, and as *Somers* tacked by nearby Pajaros Reef, his second lieutenant, James L. Parker, remarked to Semmes "that he thought it looked a little squally to windward." Semmes gave the immediate order to lower sail and "directed the helm to be put up." As he recounted in his official report on the loss of *Somers*, Semmes noted

> Lieutenant Parker took the mainsail off of her, and had got the spanker half brailed up, when the squall struck us. It did not appear to be very violent, nor was its approach accompanied by any foaming of the water, or any indications, which usually mark the approach of heavy squalls. But the brig being flying-light, having scarcely any water or provisions, and but six tons of ballast on board, was thrown over almost instantly, so far as to refuse to answer her helm.[36]

As water poured into the hatches, Semmes gave the order to take axes and chop away *Somers'* masts to try to right the ship. "But this was a forlorn hope, the brig filling very fast, and her masts and yards lying flat on the sea. . . . A few moments more, and I was convinced, in spite of all of our efforts, the brig must inevitably go down. When she was on the point of sinking beneath us, and engulfing us in the waves, I gave the order, "Every man save himself who can."[37]

Before the brig went down, the crew was able to launch a small boat, and twenty men reached Isla Verde; others grabbed on to floating wreckage, including Semmes, in a heavy sea with the wind still howling. *Somers'* boat rescued three more men, Semmes and Parker and an unnamed seaman, while other ships, foreign men-of-war observing the blockade, came to the assistance of more of *Somers'* crew in the water. Thirty-six out of the eighty-man crew, however,

FIGURE 7.2 *Somers* sinks off Veracruz

drowned. The drama and loss of *Somers* took no more than ten minutes from the time the squall struck to the rescue of the last of the survivors by boats sent by neighboring warships. Nearly half of the crew, including two officers, joined *Somers* in its watery grave. The ill-fated brig was gone. But it would never be forgotten.

Chapter 8

Legacies

The events that played out on the decks of *Somers* in December 1842, and the subsequent inquiries and Mackenzie's court-martial, had ensured persistent news coverage on a national scale that lasted for years. Even in an age of twenty-four-hour news cycles it is possible to look back at the *Somers* Affair and see it as an early example of American journalism at its sensationalist worst. Then, as with now, the news cycles ultimately played out within a few years to be revived, from time to time, as late-life reminiscences and obituaries appeared through the end of the nineteenth century with "vitiating admixtures of hearsay, confusions of detail, distortions of perspective, and egoistic reconstructions—to say nothing of hindsight."[1]

Somers and the *Somers* Affair achieved American fame, as well as infamy, through a variety of other ways. In addition to the extensive national newspaper and magazine coverage, a transcript of the court of inquiry, published in January 1843 in the New York *Weekly Tribune*, quickly was converted into an illustrated book, *Inquiry into the Somers Mutiny, with a Full Account of the Execution of Spencer, Cromwell and Small* separately published by the paper's editor, Horace Greeley. Greeley, a man of his time, was a staunch proponent of American democracy, and social and political reform. He was a defender of Alexander Slidell Mackenzie, and had earlier editorialized that Mackenzie's "prompt and fearless decision" had "frustrated and crushed . . . one of the most bold and daring conspiracies ever formed."[2] The illustrations in the *Inquiry into the Somers Mutiny* were a portrait of Mackenzie, a reproduction of Spencer's "strange characters" paper, and detailed drawings that depicted the layout of the decks and below decks areas of *Somers* as Greeley correctly assumed people wanted to get some visual sense of the stage upon which this national drama had played out. The physical reality of *Somers* had an effect on Richard Henry Dana Jr., who after touring it wrote, "You would scarcely believe your eyes if you were to see, as the scene of this dreadful conspiracy, a little brig, with low bulwarks, a single narrow deck flush fore and aft, and nothing to mark the officers' quarters. . . . You feel as though half a dozen resolute conspirators could have swept the deck and thrown overboard all that opposed them."[3]

However, the image that dominated the nation's attention was a color lithograph of *Somers* under sail, with two bodies hanging from the yardarm below a fully unfurled American flag. Published in 1843 by lithographer Nathaniel Currier, who would later be joined by James Ives to make the company *the* American image makers of the century, the *Somers* lithograph was a bestseller for a firm that gained fame as the self-advertised "Grand Central Depot for Cheap and Popular Prints." While later known for its idyllic and bucolic scenes of American life, Currier had an early penchant for dramatic scenes of disasters, wrecks, and ruins, and *Somers'* "floating gallows" fit the bill.

The drama that played out on *Somers* was fodder for reformers who ironically seized on a ship whose intended role had been reform. While the role of alcohol and sexual predation in the entire affair was by and large ignored, the concepts of unjust, un-American imposition of absolute rule before the mast, and the enforcement of that rule through violence, dominated the dialogue. The shift in attitudes against Mackenzie came not only from the shock of an extrajudicial hanging, but also from the realization that his alleged behavior was the product of a system that had enshrined despotism through brutality. At sea, as the *Somers* Affair had blatantly shown to the American public, the captain literally held the power of life and death over his crew.

Three years before the *Somers* Affair, Richard Henry Dana Jr. published *Two Years before the Mast*, an account of his time at sea as a merchant seaman. Dana had shipped as a regular hand despite his moneyed, cultured upbringing. He published his book as he began a career as a maritime lawyer. It was meant to provoke sympathy for the lot of the sailor and to rouse protests against shipboard brutality. *Two Years before the Mast* resonated; it sold 10,000 copies in its first year. In time, it became a classic of American literature. Despite his strong feelings for the rights of seamen, and his denunciation of flogging, Dana never wavered in his sympathy for Mackenzie. But another author did not share an unquestioning view of either the flogging or of the executions on *Somers*. Herman Melville, in his 1850 book *White-Jacket*, extensively described and condemned the infliction of irons and flogging as well as naval discipline and its tendency toward arbitrary and unfair punishments. That *Somers* weighed in some negative measure with Melville came with the comment in *White-Jacket* that the "well-known case of a United States brig furnishes a memorable example, which at any moment may be repeated. Three men, in a time of peace, were then hung at the yard-arm, merely because, in the Captain's judgment, it became necessary to hang them. To this day the question of their complete guilt is socially discussed."[4]

As the end of the century loomed, the topic of *Somers* returned to public consciousness with obituaries of principal players, including Alexander Slidell Mackenzie's wife Catherine in 1883, and earlier with Ambrose Spencer's 1876 murder. *Somers* also featured in late-life reminiscences, one the most powerful being Robert Rogers' published indictment of Spencer and his own memories of *Somers* and its haunted reputation. Another was an interview with widow Margaret Cromwell, then seventy-six years old and described as having lived "under the shadow of a great sorrow."[5] "Mrs. Cromwell's story differs considerably from the accounts published at the time," noted the interviewer, as she related her belief that Mackenzie, hating Spencer, had hanged Cromwell and Small because they were

Spencer's friends. Other stories rehashed the saga, some favorable to Mackenzie, others to Spencer, Cromwell, and Small; *Somers* was a perennial favorite for newspapers eager for lurid fodder. But by the end of the nineteenth century, other than rehashed stories in the press, the memory of *Somers* began to dim, even if the story was still known to naval veterans and to the fraternity brothers of Chi Psi. Chi Psi, co-founded by Philip Spencer at Union College in Schenectady, kept his memory alive, first with reminisces of "Phil," and then in the Chi Psi toast. The toast honors Spencer as an unfairly hanged brother, ending with the proclamation that "humanity suffered a blow when Philip Spencer died."

The christening of a new *Somers*, the "torpedo boat" USS *Somers* (TB-22) in 1898, the first time the navy reused the name, led to fresh publicity over an "ill-chosen name," and national stories recounted the events of "more than fifty years ago." A reminiscence from a former apprentice on the ill-fated voyage, a "Mr. K," used vivid language and took historical liberties; "the boys were told to take hold of the halyards and were told that if any one of them did not pull or if he hung back he would be shot down," and that "Spencer's box when it was thrown overboard broke in two, it being a light pine box and heavily weighted. Spencer's body fell out as the box struck the water."[6]

In the twentieth century, the name of *Somers* resurfaced nationally, as it simply was too good a story to let go. By that time, the events on the brig were avowed, in a stretch of the truth, to be the "first mutiny" and at that time the *only* mutiny in the history of the U.S. Navy. The death of Mackenzie's daughter Harriet in 1906 was one occasion for a reflection on the affair, "one of the most pathetic in the history of nations," even if "our navy has been practically exempt from any dangerous mutinous spirit during its brilliant career, with this exception."[7] Four years later, another story, syndicated to national papers, included *Somers* in a sensational recounting of "Death Examples" in the U.S. Army and Navy that were "summary executions for good of the service."[8]

The name *Somers* then went to a new naval ship, a destroyer launched from the Bethlehem Shipbuilding Corporation's San Francisco Yard in 1918 and commissioned into service in 1920. When it was decommissioned and scrapped in 1931, the name passed in time to another destroyer, USS *Somers* (DD-387), launched in 1937. It served with distinction in World War II; its last mission was, ironically, a training cruise for midshipmen in July 1945. Decommissioned in 1945 and scrapped in 1947, it passed the name *Somers* in time to a new-generation destroyer, USS *Somers* (DD-947). That *Somers*, the last for now to bear the name, was launched in 1958, converted in time to a guided missile destroyer, and decommissioned in 1988, ending its three decades of distinguished service in the Pacific (including Vietnam) before it was sunk as a target in naval exercises ten years later. It now rests, miles deep, in the Pacific off Hawai'i.

Any connection to the brig *Somers* led to a rehash of the affair: when redevelopment in September 1934 demolished 14 Lafayette Square in Washington, DC, which had been the lodgings of John Canfield Spencer and his wife, the Washington *Evening Star* devoted the heart of its real estate page to the demolished home and to *Somers'* sad tale. Ultimately, though, what made the name of the brig *Somers* famous in the twentieth century was the discovery of a lost manuscript, kept in a chest, unfinished and forgotten following the death of its author, Herman Melville. Melville's cousin was Guert Gansevoort. Plagued by his own role in the controversial events, Gansevoort had confided his doubts to some but not all and probably not to Melville.

Gansevoort's tale had inspired Melville to make mention of it in *White-Jacket*. Melville returned to the subject in his last works. The first was his poem "Billy in the Darbies," published in an 1888 volume of poetry, *John Marr and Other Sailors*, which portrays an innocent youth awaiting death by hanging in "Lone Bay," the ship's jail, his wrists secured by handcuffs, or "darbies." Poignant and powerful, it concludes with the boy lying dead on the seafloor, lashed into his hammock, and dropped overboard after his hanging.

Fathoms down, fathoms down, how I'll dream fast asleep.
I feel it stealing now. Sentry, are you there?
Just ease these darbies at the wrist,
And roll me over fair.
I am sleepy, and the oozy weeds about me twist.

Melville began a larger narrative to explain the poem, and was working on it up until a few months before he died in September 1891. Rediscovered sealed inside a tin in 1921 and finally published in 1924, the novella *Billy Budd, Sailor* resurrected the literary reputation of Herman Melville.

After the success of his earlier books based on his own South Seas adventures as a seaman, *Typee* and *Omoo*, Melville's reputation had waned. *Moby-Dick*, while now considered a classic, was roundly criticized and failed commercially when it first appeared. The discovery and publication of *Billy Budd* propelled the reputation of the long-dead author and his neglected classic, *Moby-Dick*, back into America's literary consciousness. Melville's classic relates the sad tale of Billy Budd, a seaman who was "impressed" into service when taken off his merchant ship to join the crew of the man-of-war HMS *Bellipotent*. Billy Budd is beloved by the officers and crew save one, the Master-at-Arms John Claggart, who quietly wages a campaign to impugn and undermine the seaman. When Claggart falsely accuses Billy of trying to foment mutiny, Billy, stunned and outraged, strikes Claggart with enough force to kill him. *Bellipotent*'s captain, who knows that this was an unintended act, nonetheless has to convene a quick court-martial and hangs Billy as the crew look on in horror. The epitome of youthful innocence, Billy was caught up in a naval system where absolute authority, especially in a time of war, controlled the fates of the crew, justly or unjustly. Hated by Claggart and dogged by his despotic authority, Billy was pushed beyond reason to blindly strike out and kill his tormenter—and even though the captain knew of the boy's nobility and loved Billy like a son, a love shared by the rest of the crew, the rules at sea would brook no exception. While none of the Billy Budd saga reflects what happened on *Somers*, Melville's family connection to Gansevoort, and his early criticisms of Mackenzie's actions, connected the fictional *Bellipotent* to *Somers*, Billy to Philip Spencer, and Alexander Slidell Mackenzie to Captain Vere, Billy's unwilling, but duty-bound executioner.

With *Billy Budd* came a revival of interest in the *Somers* Affair, and the entry of *Somers*' saga into a fresh cycle of debate over the fundamental questions that begin with whether Philip Spencer was a mutineer or a heedless schoolboy. Was Mackenzie justified in his actions? A decade after the publication of *Billy Budd*, readers were also reminded of another famous naval event, the mutiny on His Majesty's Armed Transport *Bounty* when in 1932 Charles Nordhoff and James Norman Hall published *Mutiny on the Bounty*, a fictional novel of that 1789 event. *Mutiny on the Bounty* was followed by two other novels by Nordhoff and Hall in 1934 that told the story of Captain Bligh's open boat voyage over a thousand miles of sea with the loyal members of his crew, and the final, fateful voyage of *Bounty* to Pitcairn Island. That in turn was followed by the epic MGM film of 1935, starring Charles Laughton as a despotic Bligh and Clark Gable as Fletcher Christian, the heroic, noble mutineer.

The Nordhoff and Hall trilogies, classics of sea literature, further revived interest in *Somers* as America's only naval "mutiny." Combined with the message of an innocent Billy Budd, the saga of *Bounty*, especially as it played out on screen in the Gable and Laughton film, which the *New York Times*' review hailed as "savagely exciting and rousingly dramatic a photoplay as has come out of Hollywood in recent years," blurred the lines, however.[9] Never mind the facts, *Somers*, Mackenzie, and Spencer were about to transition into modern American mass media culture's fascination with true crime, tragic stories, and two-dimensional depictions of complex people and situations. Alexander Slidell Mackenzie, no William

FIGURE 8.1 Movie poster for *Billy Budd*

Bligh, nonetheless came to be viewed by modern readers as *that* kind of captain. There always has to be a hero and a villain. What made the *Somers* case all the more compelling from the first mention of the news was that Mackenzie and Spencer kept changing roles throughout the inquiry, court-martial, and the years that followed. The changing mindsets of generations that followed also influenced the verdict, depending on where one stood on issues of authority and the rebelliousness of youth.

That interest blossomed further following Herman Wouk's 1951 Pulitzer Prize–winning novel, *The Caine Mutiny*, which focused on a small U.S. Navy ship, USS *Caine*, and its captain, Philip Francis Queeg, whose behavior, which seems despotic to some, is made even more intolerable as he demonstrates cowardice to his officers that he is not fit for command. When a typhoon strikes *Caine* at sea, the officers relieve Queeg of command, effectively staging a mutiny. At their court-martial, their lawyer, while disgusted with them, gets the mutineers acquitted by effectively breaking Queeg on the stand, or as he puts it, he does his job by "torpedoing" Queeg and showing up the captain's mental state. Wouk's novel inspired a 1954 Oscar-nominated film that featured Humphrey Bogart as Captain Queeg in a masterful performance. While popular, the film in particular inspired uninformed opinion and easy answers to what happened on *Somers*. The film, like the novel, was itself ambiguous, and focused on the interpersonal relationships, suggesting to some that Mackenzie may have been unbalanced. To that point, the producers offered an onscreen line after the opening credits of *The Caine Mutiny* that read: "There has never been a mutiny in a ship of the United States Navy. The truths of this film lie not in its incidents, but in the way a few men meet the crisis of their lives." For Spencer partisans, this was a posthumous indictment of Mackenzie, as there had been no mutiny on *Somers*.

In 1954, journalist Frederick Franklyn Van de Water, formerly with the *New York Tribune*, an early investigative reporter for *Harper's* and *Colliers*, and author of thirty-four books, published the first modern account of *Somers, The Captain Called It Mutiny*. It was in part based on family stories, as Van de Water was "the descendant of a 17-year-old sailor who was imprisoned on board the *Somers*." *Time* magazine's review noted that it was the story of "Queeg's Predecessor." Van de Water noted in his foreword how it is human instinct "to overlook matters that resist neat explanations," but plainly focused on "certain fundamentals that deny the existence of a mutiny."[10]

Van de Water's verdict that Mackenzie had overreacted to Spencer's exceptionally rash acts of insubordination was playacting on a dangerous subject. Mackenzie was ultimately a "phenomenally self-righteous man . . . sure of his rectitude, as only an intensely vain, completely humorless man could be." Philip Spencer was a "sulky incorrigible."[11] That somehow rings kinder than sailor historian Samuel Eliot Morison's judgment, also written around that time, that Spencer was a "prototype of what nowadays is called a 'young punk.'" While the idea that Mackenzie might have not quickly executed the three men was a "teasing thought" for Morison, his actions were "morally, if not legally" justified. For Morison, the thought of seeking justice ashore was too dangerous, and "every man on board with maritime experience and proved loyalty believed the execution was necessary." The fault, for Morison, was Spencer's, as well as the system that placed him on *Somers*, and since the founding of the Naval Academy, with its "discipline . . . such that nobody even remotely resembling Philip Spencer has since obtained a naval commission."[12] Not so for Frederick Van de Water. Spencer and Mackenzie were each "in his own way . . . so fallible that it is impossible completely to justify either." Van de Water's thoughtful, ambiguous, and compelling book was followed by a scholarly compendium of original documents, published in 1959 by Melville scholar Harrison Hayford. It was a landmark offering of original sources from the nineteenth century, starting from the breaking news cycle through to the era where *Somers* passed into memory and then into modern times.

In 1972, a novel by Henry Carlisle, *Voyage to the First of December*, once again reminded non-Melville-reading Americans of the *Somers*. Described as a "taut novel" in a *Time* magazine review, *Voyage to the First of December* was hailed as a "great success" in looking at the characters of Mackenzie and Spencer, as seen through the eyes of Surgeon Leecock. It provoked reviewer Thomas Carmichael to note that it was almost impossible to read the account of the executions "without believing you are actually there." The book was a fictional work, drawing on the published accounts of the time, with no real journal of surgeon "Robert Leacock," and in it, Mackenzie and his officers do not fare well. Carlisle, writing in the era of Vietnam and changing attitudes to military authority, blamed the affair on Mackenzie's inept leadership and fatally misunderstanding the "childish games" of Spencer. Cromwell and Small were "innocents caught up in the unfolding tragedy." The book ends with the surgeon committing suicide because Mackenzie has shifted some of the blame to him, and that *Somers* was haunted, and "sometimes the laughter of Philip Spencer echoed in the rigging."[13]

Epilogue

As sometimes happens with incredible sea stories that involve a shipwreck, the vessel itself was found in its undisturbed watery grave in 1986. The discovery of the remains of *Somers* called to mind the powerful, if not accurate comment at the beginning of Henry Carlisle's book that for more than a century, "the affair languished in near-oblivion, submerged in history like a forgotten wreck, its presence marked on old charts, its full truth never salvaged."[1] For those who seek the tangible traces of the past, words like that are a challenge. Texas-born adventurer and art dealer George Belcher took up the challenge. Growing up on the banks of the Rio Grande in McAllen, Texas, young Belcher was a frequent visitor to Mexico. The new McAllen-Hidalgo-Reynosa International Bridge opened in 1941, the year of his birth. The bridge spurred the development of the region in both countries, and McAllen boomed. Belcher's first international travels were across that bridge. A fluent Spanish speaker, Belcher retained a strong love of Mexico, its people and culture, and for many years specialized in the marketing and sale of Mexican art.

After graduating from the University of Texas in 1964, Belcher joined the Peace Corps and spent two years in Bolivia before shifting to the newly established U.S. Agency for International Development (USAID) in 1967 and heading to Vietnam. For his first two years, Belcher worked closely with the South Vietnamese military in the Mekong Delta as part of Chiêu Hồi, a program devoted to encouraging North Vietnamese and Viet Cong soldiers to defect to the South.

In 1969, Belcher took leave to see more of the world and engage in adventure. In time, he moved from Honolulu to San Francisco, ran an art gallery for a year, and then opened his own gallery in 1975, focusing on Mexican art and paintings. In his first year in San Francisco, loving old books and first editions, he was offered a copy of Raphael Semmes' autobiographical account of his service in the Mexican War at "an affordable price," he later noted. In its pages, he read of *Somers* and its loss, and was inspired someday to go to Veracruz and find the wreck.

That opportunity came through his sale of a painting by José Maria Velasco through a Mexican art agent to a client in Mexico in 1983. The client turned out to be the governor of Xalapa State. Agustin Acosta Lagunes hired Belcher to acquire more art and artifacts in the United States for the Museo de Antropología de Xalapa. The following year, Belcher convinced Acosta Lagunes that a funded search for *Somers* and other wrecks could add interesting artifacts— and maybe some Spanish treasure—to the museum's displays. With official permission, Belcher set out, but his first year's effort failed to find the wreck in 1985. The discovery (pre-Internet) of an 1846 map of Mexico that clearly showed the location where *Somers* sank renewed the search, so Belcher returned with his brother Joel in June 1986 to start again, towing a magnetometer (an instrument that detects variations in the Earth's magnetic field and a tool regularly used to locate shipwrecks) behind a rented boat. They were nearing the end of one long line as their boat ran a gridded pattern to "mow the lawn" on June 2 when the weather changed, and a sudden rain squall sprang up, obscuring the sea and nearly swamping their boat. As the wind howled and rain beat down, they started to head for Isla Verde for shelter when the magnetometer recorded a faint signature that might be a shipwreck. At that point, the storm ended. The Belcher brothers quickly donned their dive gear and dropped into the sea:

Joel and I swam down into a dark green sea that seemed to get darker and darker as we got deeper. It seemed as if we were swimming down through a tunnel; however it was strange that when we neared the bottom, there was a glow because the sand was reflecting back the little light that had made it down over one hundred feet. As Joel and I arrived at the bottom, we were amazed to see in the heart of that glow the half-buried bones of the brig *Somers*. We had come down right on top . . . the brig *Somers* had been a real ship, crewed by real men, thirty-two of whom died when she died.[2]

The wreck lay in 107 feet of water, its hull outlined by the corroded green of its copper-sheathed timbers, and filled with a jumble of artifacts. The Belchers were the first people to see *Somers* in nearly a century and a half.

He brought in archaeologist Mitchell "Mitch" Marken from the United States on a return to the wreck in October 1986. Marken did a map of the wreck site, a key step in archaeological investigation, and after the mapping, Belcher recovered a few brass ship's spikes, a bottle, and two ceramic jars that once held provisions. The bottle, with a foil cap, had the imprint of Wells, Miller & Provost of 217 Front Street, New York. They were pickles, bottled preserves, and sauce merchants. The name of the company on the bottle dated it to after 1844, when John B. Wells and Ebenezer Miller were joined in the business by Stephen H. Provost. They were regular suppliers to the U.S. Navy. One of the stoneware jars was embossed with the name of Benedict Milburn of Alexandria, DC. Alexandria, Virginia, had been part of the District of Columbia from 1789 to 1846, and Milburn had been active between 1825 and 1842 in Alexandria.

George Belcher and Mitch Marken were sure—98 percent sure, he later said—that the wreck was *Somers*. They needed another archaeologist's opinion, and at that, an archaeologist hopefully with the U.S. government, as Belcher believed the next step was to get the government interested in this historic shipwreck in Mexican waters, ideally the U.S. Navy. They settled for the National Park Service

FIGURE E.1 George Belcher on the wreck of *Somers*, 1987

when Marken sat next to me in a session on the historic wreck USS *Monitor* at the Society for Historical Archaeology's January 1987 meeting, that year held in Savannah, Georgia. I was then serving as the head of the National Maritime Initiative, the de facto national maritime preservation program, as the maritime historian of the National Park Service in Washington, DC. We'd just finished a series of studies that led to *Monitor*'s being designated a national historic landmark, and Mitch was full of questions about naval wrecks and protecting them, especially very significant ones. He asked if I would mind speaking with a friend who had found a then unnamed historic navy wreck, so we went up to his room, where he placed a call, chatted for a couple of minutes, and then handed me the phone. George Belcher was at the other end.

The discussion was fascinating, and Belcher shared details that made it clear that this wreck was likely *Somers*. He suggested, when I returned to Washington, DC, that I meet with an old friend of his from Peace Corps days in Bolivia, Robert S. "Bob" Gelbard. Gelbard was at that time, having joined the State Department in 1967, the deputy assistant secretary of state for South America. With his interest and support for a more formal U.S. government assessment of Belcher's find, I discussed the probable find with my boss, NPS chief historian Edwin C. Bearss, and we also talked with the Naval Historical Center, then headed by Ronald H. Spector and the navy's chief historian, William S. "Bill" Dudley. We agreed that a look was necessary, so on official leave, I went to Mexico as Belcher's guest to dive on the wreck in late May 1987, nearly a year after the discovery.

In Veracruz, Belcher, his brother Joel, Marken, filmmaker Marty Snyderman and his assistant Chip Matheson, and I dived on the wreck from May 27 to June 5. The wreck was as dramatically laid out in the sand as George Belcher had described. As we dropped to a hundred feet, we hit a deep depression, and at the bottom of it were the copper-clad bones of the wreck. Currents had scoured around the wreck, settling it deeper into the seabed. At some point, the wreck would have ultimately been buried without a trace. My job was to confirm the identity of the wreck. After a long dive and a series of observations, it was clear that it was *Somers*; the dimensions of the wreck matched those recorded for *Somers*, and the outline of the hull, with a sharp, clipper bow and stern, was prominently defined. The wreck lay over on its starboard side, the position of *Somers* when it capsized. There were the same type of guns, 32-pdr. carronades, and only them, on the wreck, and small arms, including cutlasses, and a U.S. Navy chronometer, used in navigation, lay near the stern where the helm had once been. Time and the power of the sea had both taken away portions of the wreck while preserving other parts of the brig.

The lower hull survived as a fragile shell where the worms stopped eating as they encountered the metal, which is toxic to them. Laid out in the sand, both inside and outside of the wreck, was an array of all that was on and in *Somers* that fell to the seabed as the brig decayed and fell apart. Lying in perfect, undisturbed order were the anchors, just off the bow, the windlass at the bow, stowed anchor chain that lay in neat rows, the galley stove, the metal tubes of the ship's pumps, wardroom china, bottles, and the glass panes from the wardroom skylight, with the tiller, the remains of two arms chests with the small arms and cutlasses, and then the rudder. Mitch Marken laid out a baseline that we used to measure and map the wreck to add to his earlier work. With the Belcher brothers, we swam out, past the hull, and on the sand found the remains of the rigging, laid out on the seabed. There lay the remains of the blocks and rigging tackle. This was all that was left of the yards from which the three men were hanged. They lay in the sand, still oriented as if on the now-vanished spars. I made sketches with pencil on frosted Mylar (one of the "tricks of the trade" for underwater archaeologists who need to make notes) of one of the carronades, which was in the position of the gun marked on contemporary plans as the one that Spencer had been chained next to. It was surreal, in a sense. Everything on the seabed, in and around the wreck, matched the position of gear and compartments noted on the simple plans published by Horace Greeley to share the layout of *Somers* to the public in 1843. At little more than a hundred feet in length, and narrow, the small size of *Somers* was a shock when you floated over it and considered how crowded those decks must have been and how terrified a captain would feel if he had suspected a mutiny, a point made by Richard Henry Dana when he visited the brig at anchor at the New York Navy Yard.

Throughout my career in dealing with shipwrecks, the subject of ghosts and hauntings has always been a topic of discussion. My first shipwreck project, with the broken hulk of the wooden steamship *Tennessee* that went ashore north of the Golden Gate in 1853, introduced me to what was supposedly a "ghost ship," reappearing on foggy mornings. All I ever saw were scattered fragments of the steamer mixed into the sand. Since then, I've dived on and investigated countless shipwrecks, some of them tragic ships with significant loss of life, including USS *Arizona* at Pearl Harbor and *Titanic*. Not once did I ever feel or see anything other than the physical testimony of what had happened to those ships and those on board, but no ghosts. Only once have I had a paranormal "encounter" and that was on *Somers*.

Something I have not spoken of publicly, until now, is the sense you have on that wreck. It came in the dark, when you were swimming alone, that there was a presence near you. Thinking it was another diver approaching in the murk, you would turn, and see no one there. We'd all scoffed at the tale of the night aloft and the crew's belief that the three dead men's ghosts were still hanging from the yardarms. We continued to scoff until at the end of one day, as we left the bottom, Chip Matheson remained behind to gather up the lights and cables from the underwater filming and follow the rest of the group up. The phrase "ghost ship" had often been tossed round as we sat on the boat after each dive, but that was as much an observation about how much the wreck looked like the skeleton of the ship it had once been as opposed to a discussion of Rogers' 1890 tale of a haunted ship. When Matheson surfaced from his decompression, he was angry. He had circled the wreck, picking up loose lines and gear. In the murk, he thought he could see someone else, just out of full view. As he worked, the other person followed, and he could hear them yelling something through the water. The yelling finally stopped, and he finished his work, and seeing no one else on the site, he headed up, hanging on the decompression line for a half hour.

The time spent at 107 feet meant every diver had to hang on the line at 30, 20, and then 10 feet to slowly decompress in order to prevent the bends. We all dreaded it, as Veracruz had a few dozen open sewers that emptied into the bay, and even miles out, that which floated by was less than savory. You had to decompress using a spare air tank hanging from the end of a line, which meant taking your regulator out and put that tank's regulator in. Needless to say, we were all eager to be out of the water and on the dive boat. Chip came up the line and stared angrily at us as we hung there; we were the first up, having preceded him by several minutes. When he surfaced, still floating off the boat, he started yelling. Which one of us, he demanded, had followed behind him shouting at him as he gathered up the lighting gear? We laughed, and he got angrier. It was then that we knew this was not a joke, and Chip realized he'd been down there alone. We all grew silent. When he'd been down there, Chip was *alone* on the wreck during the time he had his encounter.

The announcement of the discovery, in 1987, was in time followed by diplomatic negotiations with Mexico to protect it as a war grave and as a historic and archaeological site. I was part of the U.S. delegation that opened the negotiations. It was a sensitive matter, as *Somers* was lost in a war in which the United States seized over *half* of Mexico's territory in the name of Manifest Destiny. Mexico disagreed with the U.S. position that all warships, whether afloat or sunk, remain the sovereign property of the nation that they had served. They argued that Mexico had sunk *Somers* during the war, and thus gained ownership. We finally came to an agreement at the suggestion of Captain Ash Roach, U.S.N. (Ret.), then a lawyer with the State Department's Office of Ocean Law and Policy, who accompanied me for the initial negotiations in Mexico City. Ash suggested, and we all shook hands on, the decision to agree to disagree and get on with both nations formally and officially assessing the wreck. Nothing about the brig *Somers* was or is easy, and controversy around the wreck continued even at the end of the twentieth century.

News of the discovery of the wreck made national and international news when we announced it at a San Francisco press conference in November 1987. With headlines like "Wreck of the Warship That Inspired 'Billy Budd' Discovered off Mexico," *Somers* was again in the news. With that came pressure to "protect" the wreck, as Belcher's experience with the treasure hunters and the keen interest of Veracruz-based divers and relic collectors convinced him that *Somers* not only could but would be pillaged. Various discussions between the National Park Service, the Naval Historical Center (which has since been renamed the Naval History and Heritage Command), the Department of State, and Pilar Luna Erreguerena, the head of Mexico's underwater archaeological branch within the Instituto Nacional de Antropología e Historia in Mexico City, followed. To help nudge things along, because U.S. senator Howell Heflin (D-Alabama) had expressed a strong interest in the U.S. taking a stance on its ownership of the Confederate raider CSS *Alabama*, sunk off Cherbourg, France, in 1864, and encouraged international cooperation, I was able, at Ed Bearss' suggestion, to sit down with the senator's staff and draft a bill for the 100th Congress, 2nd Session to consider. S-2736 was written "to urge negotiations with the Government of Mexico for the preservation and study of the wreck of the USS *Somers*."

The bill incorporated the views and policies of the navy, and was in accord with U.S. law and policy. It was introduced on August 11, 1988, read twice and referred to the Committee on Foreign Relations. It did not need to pass; it helped show the executive branch of the government that the senator had an interest in Raphael Semmes' onetime, ill-fated command now that it had been found at the bottom of the sea. That was all it took for the negotiations to proceed to their final agreement to disagree but to also get out to formally examine and more thoroughly document the wreck. In July 1990, with fellow NPS archaeologists Larry Nordby, Jerry Livingston, and John Brooks, and joined by the Belchers; Mexico's head of underwater archaeology, the late Pilar Luna Erreguerena, and her archaeological team of Santiago Analco and Juan Rique; and a team of eight Mexican Navy divers headed by Captain Juan Enrique Suarez Paredo Navarette, we completed a detailed assessment and mapping of the wreck of *Somers*.

We worked from the Mexican navy patrol boat *Margarita Maza de Juarez*, commanded by Captain Santos Gómez Leyva, to document not only the physical remains of an infamous vessel, but also a war grave and historic site that no one was legally allowed to visit. However, it was discovered on the first dive that local divers had looted the wreck, taking artifacts and damaging the fragile remains of the hull. Many features remained, however, and among the new observations were the davits for the twenty-foot-long port quarter boat, the only one of *Somers'* boats to get clear of the wreck and rescue survivors when the brig sank. Luna and I probed the muzzles of the carronades and we found solid obstructions in two of the guns that suggested they were loaded; this made sense considering *Somers* was on blockade duty and was about to stop a suspected blockade runner when the squall hit. A sobering moment came when at the bow divers encountered a scatter of bones; too large to be human, which was the divers' initial thoughts, they were all that remained from salted meat provisions. It was nonetheless a reminder that this was a grave, but no human remains have been seen at the site or recovered from it.

The project was successful; it was the first international underwater archaeological project conducted jointly by the United States with another government outside of the former Trust Territories in the Pacific. The gracious commitment and expertise of the people of Mexico to examine a ship lost in a war that is still remembered as the "First War of North American Intervention" spoke volumes to the power of reconciliation in modern times. Also key, and not to be forgotten, is that when George and Joel Belcher discovered the wreck, on their own time and with their own money, they did not attempt to plunder it for profit, but worked at considerable personal expense to see the wreck studied and protected. They joined every expedition, and with the 1990 expedition, were able to symbolically transfer responsibility for the wreck to its appropriate keepers. Work on *Somers* continues into the twenty-first century, with a recent Mexican expedition using the latest modern technology to document the wreck.[3]

The looting of the wreck between the time of its discovery and the ability of the two governments to mobilize the first expedition in 1990 in no way diminished the contribution or the legacy of the most infamous ship in the history of the U.S. Navy. The lost warships in the oceans and lakes are a vast museum of history, and *Somers'* survival as an archaeological site off Veracruz speaks powerfully to that point. Mexico and Mexican archaeologists and historians followed the 1990 project with dives and assessments, and that included another joint Mexican and U.S. team from the National Park Service, INAH, and the Armada de Mexico who again assessed *Somers* in 1999 and updated the archaeological map of the site. *Somers* is now protected by Mexican law through the international agreement. It is seen as a significant reminder of a difficult joint cultural heritage. Even reminders of less happy past events are significant, whether they be the events of December 1, 1842, the subsequent controversies, or a war between the two nations that left *Somers* below the waves.

The wreck is no longer readily accessible, as changing shipping lanes now place the site in a no-dive area along the approaches to a busy port. Special permission is required to dive, if absolutely necessary, because the harbor master has to stop ships from crossing over the site. And so *Somers*, too fragile to be raised, and alone with its ghosts, be they real or imagined, is again left to the sea.

NOTES

Chapter 1

1. New York *Weekly Tribune*, January 21, 1843.

2. Child, *Gazetteer and Business Directory of Ontario County*, 39.

3. The size and population are from Milliken, *A History of Ontario County, New York and Its People*, 272.

4. Fessenden, *Genealogical Story*, ii.

5. Rochester, New York, *Democrat and Chronicle*, December 25, 1900.

6. Fessenden, *Genealogical Story*, 39.

7. Rochester, New York, *Democrat and Chronicle*, December 25, 1900.

8. Jennie Lee, *My Life with Nye*, 196.

9. Rochester, New York, *Democrat and Chronicle*, December 25, 1900.

10. *National Encyclopaedia of American Biography*, vol. 6, 6–7.

11. *The Diary of Philip Hone*, vol. 2, 165.

12. Rochester, New York, *Democrat and Chronicle*, December 25, 1900.

13. Vaughan, *The Antimasonic Party in the United States*, 1.

14. Letter from Daniel Webster to Ambrose Spencer, November 16, 1831, reproduced in Webster, *The Writings and Speeches of Daniel Webster*, vol. 4, 215.

15. Spencer, *American Institutions and Their Influence by Alexis de Tocqueville*, 229.

16. Howe, "My Schools and Scholars. No. IV," 23–31.

17. Post, *Observations on the Cure of Strabismus*, 13.

18. Howe, "My Schools and Scholars," 23–31.

19. Slifer and Kennicott, *The Chi Psi Story*, 74.

20. Howe, "My Schools and Scholars," 24.

21. Ellms, *The Pirates Own Book*, 3.

22. Howe, "My Schools and Scholars," 24.

23. The reminiscences of Spencer penned by classmate Paul F. Cooper and others appeared in the Chi Psi journal *The Purple and Gold* in April 1885 and are reproduced in Hayford, *The Somers Mutiny Affair*, 208.

24. The quotes are from are from *The Purple and Gold* reminiscent account of Spencer published in April 1885 and reproduced in Hayford, *The Somers Mutiny Affair*, 208.

25. The disciplinary records cited by Professor Charles D. Vail are from are also from *The Purple and Gold* reminiscent account of Spencer published in April 1885 and reproduced in Hayford, *The Somers Mutiny Affair*, 208.

26. Howe, "My Schools and Scholars," 26.

27. The "Patriarch of the Freshman Class" incident is from Gay 1951, 71, 74–75, and is also in White (1905), vol. 1, 17–18.

28. From reminiscences of Spencer in the Chi Psi journal *The Purple and Gold* in April 1885 and reproduced in Hayford, *The Somers Mutiny Affair*, 208.

29. The strabismus surgical procedure is from Post, *Observations on the Cure of Strabismus*, 16–17, 20–24, 29.

30. From *The Purple and Gold* reminiscent account of Spencer published in April 1885 and reproduced in Hayford, *The Somers Mutiny Affair*, 208.

31. Howe, "My Schools and Scholars," 27.

32. The memories of Spencer are from *The Purple and Gold* reminiscent account of Spencer published in April 1885 and reproduced in Hayford, *The Somers Mutiny Affair*, 208.

33. Howe, "My Schools and Scholars," 24.

34. From an account in the Batavia, New York, *The Spirit of the Times*, January 3, 1843.

35. From the account in the Batavia, New York, *The Spirit of the Times*, January 3, 1843.

36. From the account in the Batavia, New York, *The Spirit of the Times*, January 3, 1843.

37. Howe, "My Schools and Scholars," 27.

38. Craney's story is from Adams, *Richard Henry Dana*, vol. 1, 59–63.

39. Seward's comment is from Seward, *William H. Seward*, 640.

40. Rogers' reminiscences were published in the *United Service*, 23–36.

41. From Mackenzie's letter of December 19, 1842, to Secretary of the Navy Abel Upshur, in *Proceedings of the Naval Court-Martial in the Case against Alexander Slidell Mackenzie* (hereafter cited as *Proceedings of the Naval Court-Martial*), 196.

Chapter 2

1. Paullin, "Dueling in the Old Navy," 1163.

2. Mackenzie, *Life of Stephen Decatur*, 16.

3. Chapelle, *The History of the American Sailing Navy*, 430.

4. *Boston Post*, May 21, 1842.

5. Longworth, *New-York City Directory, 1803/1804*, 263.

6. Dickens, "Over the Ways Story," 418.

7. Gouverneur, *As I Remember*, 94.

8. Barrett, *The Old Merchants of New York City*, 257, 260.

9. Irving, *Washington Irving*, vol. 2, 79, 197.

10. "Ticknor's Spanish Literature," 295.

11. Lawrence J. Friedman and David Curtis Skaggs in "Jesse Duncan Elliott and the Battle of Lake Erie" discuss the background of the feud and the subsequent controversies.

12. Lounsbury, *American Men of Letters: James Fennimore Cooper*, 213.

13. Washington, DC, *The Madisonian*, June 14, 1843.

14. Lever, *The Young Sea Officer's Sheet Anchor*, 1.

15. Biddlecomb, *The Art of Rigging*, 109.

16. *Chicago Tribune*, August 26, 1863.

17. Complaints about *Somers*' rig were many; the summary of the Mackenzie court-martial makes the point that the brig was "unsuited for such a crew," in *Proceedings of the Naval Court-Martial*, 333.

18. Bradford, ed., *Command under Sail*, i.

19. Paullin, *Commodore John Rodgers, Captain, Commodore, and Senior Officer of the American Navy, 1773–1838*, 383.

20. "Trade of Porto Rico," *Simmonds's Colonial Magazine and Foreign Miscellany*, Vol. 2, No. 5, May 1844, 103–104.

21. *Proceedings of the Naval Court-Martial*, 183.

22. New York *Evening Post*, August 11, 1842, 2.

23. Testimony of Purser Heiskill, in *Proceedings of the Naval Court-Martial*, 162.

24. New York *Evening Post*, January 11, 1843.

25. The story of *Grampus* and *Palmyra* is from the Charleston *Daily Courier*, October 9, 1822.

26. Charleston *Daily Courier*, June 26, 1843.

Chapter 3

1. I principally relied on Howe, *What Hath God Wrought*.

2. The synopsis of American immigration and its tensions is drawn in part from Oakes et al., *Of the People*, and Miller, *Emigrants and Exiles*.

3. Howe, *What Hath God Wrought*, 173.

4. Carwardine, *Evangelicals and Politics in Antebellum America*, 44.

5. Edwards, "Religious Forces in the United States, 1815–1830," 435, 436.

6. There are a number of excellent works on the various reform movements of the time; I drew mainly from Mintz, *Moralists and Modernizers*, and Walters, *American Reformers, 1815–1860*.

7. Rorabaugh, *The Alcoholic Republic*, 21, 144.

8. *Diary of Philip Hone*, vol. 1, 485.

9. The classic reference is Harold D. Langley's *Social Reform in the United States Navy, 1789–1862* (1967).

10. These quotes are from Spencer's obituary in the Albany *Morning Express*, May 19, 1855.

11. See Karp, "Slavery and American Sea Power," 288–289.

12. *Report of the Secretary of the Navy*, 1841, 374–375.

13. Jackson's farewell address of March 4, 1837, as reproduced in Richardson, *A Compilation of the Messages and Papers of the Presidents*, Vol. III, 307.

14. McNally, *Evils and Abuses in the Naval and Merchant Service, Exposed*, 156.

15. "A Glimpse at Our Navy," *The Advocate of Peace*, pp. 189–190.

16. Glenn, *Jack Tar's Story*, 116. Glenn's research found McNally serving as a ship's boy on USS *Fairfield* from 1828 to 1829, 125.

17. Dana, *Two Years before the Mast, and Twenty-Four Years After*, 104.

18. "The Moral Character of the Navy," *The Advocate of Peace*, 186–187.

19. Horner, *The Diseases and Injuries of Seamen*, 96–97.

20. Beach, *The United States Navy*, 179.

21. *The Report of the Secretary of the Navy*, 1841, 385.

Chapter 4

1. This point is made in Goldberg, "The *Somers* Mutiny," 127.

2. Nordhoff, *Man-of-War Life*, 73.

3. Goldberg, "The *Somers* Mutiny," 149.

4. This is drawn from current policy language, but the rules remain pertinent and same; see Powers, "Navy Fraternization Policies."

5. Purser Wales' testimony, in *Proceedings of the Naval Court-Martial*, 16.

6. Purser Wales' testimony, in *Proceedings of the Naval Court-Martial*, 15.

7. Matthew Calbraith Perry Jr.'s testimony, in *Proceedings of the Naval Court-Martial*, 70.

8. Midshipman Henry Rogers' testimony, in *Proceedings of the Naval Court-Martial*, 129.

9. Dana, *Two Years before the Mast*, 75.

10. Lieutenant Gansevoort's testimony, in *Proceedings of the Naval Court-Martial*, 54, 56.

11. Lieutenant Gansevoort's testimony, in *Proceedings of the Naval Court-Martial*, 54, 56.

12. Lieutenant Gansevoort's testimony, in *Proceedings of the Naval Court-Martial*, 54, 56.

13. Midshipman Tillotson's testimony, in *Proceedings of the Naval Court-Martial*, 55.

14. Purser Wales' testimony, in *Proceedings of the Naval Court-Martial*, 14.

15. *Somers'* punishment log was published in the New York *Tribune* of January 14, 1843, 1. Benemann discusses the term as a metaphor and punishment for it in *Unruly Desires*, 155, 219.

16. Seaman Neville's testimony, in *Proceedings of the Naval Court-Martial*, 80.

17. Midshipman Thompson's testimony, in *Proceedings of the Naval Court-Martial*, 188.

18. Egan, *Every Gentleman's Manual*, 9.

19. Purser Wales' testimony, in *Proceedings of the Naval Court-Martial*, 14.

20. Burg, *The Erotic Diaries of Philip C. Van Buskirk*, 26–27, 73, 77. Benemann discusses and contextualizes Van Buskirk's activities in *Unruly Desires*, 5–11, *passim*.

21. Seaman Neville's testimony, in *Proceedings of the Naval Court-Martial*, 27.

22. Benemann, *Unruly Desires*, 27–28. Benemann makes several points on tattooing as part of joining a brotherhood, and Melville's double entendre use of pricking, 29, 50.

23. Melville, *White-Jacket*, 74.

24. Seaman Neville's testimony, in *Proceedings of the Naval Court-Martial*, 80, 81.

25. Apprentice Green's testimony, in *Proceedings of the Naval Court-Martial*, 219. The portrait appears on page 3 of *The Pirates Own Book*.

26. Apprentice Snyder's testimony, in *Proceedings of the Naval Court-Martial*, 224.

27. Apprentice English's testimony, in *Proceedings of the Naval Court-Martial*, 84.

28. Apprentice Inglis' testimony, in *Proceedings of the Naval Court-Martial*, 107.

29. Sergeant-at-Arms Garty's testimony, in *Proceedings of the Naval Court-Martial*, 119.

30. The conversation between the two summarized here is from Purser Wales' testimony, in *Proceedings of the Naval Court-Martial*, 10–12.

31. Purser Wales' testimony, in *Proceedings of the Naval Court-Martial*, 11.

32. Apprentice Tyson's testimony, in *Proceedings of the Naval Court-Martial*, 113.

33. The conversation between Mackenzie and Spencer is recounted in Mackenzie's letter to Upshur of December 19, 1842, reproduced in *Proceedings of the Naval Court-Martial*, 194–197.

34. Mackenzie's letter to Secretary Upshur, in *Proceedings of the Naval Court-Martial*, 197.

Chapter 5

1. Mackenzie's letter to Secretary Upshur, in *Proceedings of the Naval Court-Martial*, 195.

2. Lieutenant Gansevoort's testimony, in *Proceedings of the Naval Court-Martial*, 32.

3. Purser Wales' testimony, in *Proceedings of the Naval Court-Martial*, 11.

4. Mackenzie's letter to Secretary Upshur, in *Proceedings of the Naval Court-Martial*, 198.

5. A reproduction of Spencer's papers, in *Proceedings of the Naval Court-Martial*, appendix, 129.

6. Mackenzie's letter to Secretary Upshur, in *Proceedings of the Naval Court-Martial*, 197.

7. Apprentice King's testimony, in *Proceedings of the Naval Court-Martial*, 145.

8. Mackenzie's letter to Secretary Upshur, in *Proceedings of the Naval Court-Martial*, 198–199.

9. Mackenzie's letter to Secretary Upshur, in *Proceedings of the Naval Court-Martial*, 191.

10. Apprentice Tyson's testimony, in *Proceedings of the Naval Court-Martial*, 111.

11. Lieutenant Gansevoort's testimony, in *Proceedings of the Naval Court-Martial*, 48.

12. Purser Wales' testimony, in *Proceedings of the Naval Court-Martial*, 16.

13. Lieutenant Gansevoort's testimony, in *Proceedings of the Naval Court-Martial*, 37.

14. Lieutenant Gansevoort's testimony, in *Proceedings of the Naval Court-Martial*, 38.

15. Mackenzie's letter to Secretary Upshur, in *Proceedings of the Naval Court-Martial*, 199.

16. Mackenzie's letter to Secretary Upshur, in *Proceedings of the Naval Court-Martial*, 199–200.

17. Mackenzie's letter to Secretary Upshur, in *Proceedings of the Naval Court-Martial*, 199–200.

18. Mackenzie's letter to Secretary Upshur, in *Proceedings of the Naval Court-Martial*, 197.

19. Apprentice King's testimony, in answer to a question from the Judge Advocate, in *Proceedings of the Naval Court-Martial*, 139.

20. Apprentice Humbert's testimony, in *Proceedings of the Naval Court-Martial*, 101.

21. Landsman McKinley's testimony, in *Proceedings of the Naval Court-Martial*, 179.

22. Apprentice King's testimony, in *Proceedings of the Naval Court-Martial*, 139.

23. Mackenzie's letter to Secretary Upshur, in *Proceedings of the Naval Court-Martial*, 201.

24. Landman McKinley's testimony, in *Proceedings of the Naval Court-Martial*, 179.

25. Landman McKinley's testimony, in *Proceedings of the Naval Court-Martial*, 178.

26. Lieutenant Gansevoort's testimony, in *Proceedings of the Naval Court-Martial*, 33.

27. Mackenzie's letter to Secretary Upshur, in *Proceedings of the Naval Court-Martial*, 201.

28. Mackenzie's letter to his officers, in *Proceedings of the Naval Court-Martial*, 33.

29. Mackenzie's letter to Secretary Upshur, in *Proceedings of the Naval Court-Martial*, 196.

30. Remarks of William H. Norris, judge advocate, in *Proceedings of the Naval Court-Martial*, 35.

31. Mackenzie's letter to Secretary Upshur, in *Proceedings of the Naval Court-Martial*, 193.

32. Lieutenant Gansevoort's testimony, in *Proceedings of the Naval Court-Martial*, 41.

33. Lieutenant Gansevoort's testimony, in *Proceedings of the Naval Court-Martial*, 49.

34. Lieutenant Gansevoort's testimony, in *Proceedings of the Naval Court-Martial*, 51.

35. Surgeon Leecock's testimony, in *Proceedings of the Naval Court-Martial*, 220.

36. Andrew Anderson's testimony to the officers' tribunal on *Somers*, cited in *Proceedings of the Naval Court-Martial*, 154.

37. Mackenzie's letter to Secretary Upshur, in *Proceedings of the Naval Court-Martial*, 202–203.

38. Mackenzie's letter to Secretary Upshur, in *Proceedings of the Naval Court-Martial*, 203.

39. Mackenzie's letter to Secretary Upshur, in *Proceedings of the Naval Court-Martial*, 203.

40. What Cromwell *might* have been reading was "Froissart and His Chronicle, No. VI," 353.

41. Mackenzie's letter to Secretary Upshur, in *Proceedings of the Naval Court-Martial*, 203.

42. Mackenzie's letter to Secretary Upshur, in *Proceedings of the Naval Court-Martial*, 204.

43. Mackenzie's letter to Secretary Upshur, in *Proceedings of the Naval Court-Martial*, 205.

44. McFarland, *Sea Dangers*, 142.

45. Mackenzie's letter to Secretary Upshur, in *Proceedings of the Naval Court-Martial*, 204, 205.

46. Mackenzie's letter to Secretary Upshur, in *Proceedings of the Naval Court-Martial*, 204, 205.

47. Mackenzie's letter to Secretary Upshur, in *Proceedings of the Naval Court-Martial*, 205.

48. Mackenzie's letter to Secretary Upshur, in *Proceedings of the Naval Court-Martial*, 204.

49. Mackenzie's letter to Secretary Upshur, in *Proceedings of the Naval Court-Martial*, 205.

50. Mackenzie's cross-examination question to apprentice Conger after his testimony, in *Proceedings of the Naval Court-Martial*, 128.

51. Mackenzie's letter to Secretary Upshur, in *Proceedings of the Naval Court-Martial*, 206.

52. Mackenzie's letter to Secretary Upshur, in *Proceedings of the Naval Court-Martial*, 206–207. Unlike modern usage, Small would not have used the term "bugger" lightly. Both men knew what he was saying.

53. Mackenzie's letter to Secretary Upshur, in *Proceedings of the Naval Court-Martial*, 207.

54. Mackenzie's letter to Secretary Upshur, in *Proceedings of the Naval Court-Martial*, 207.

55. Purser Heiskell's testimony, in *Proceedings of the Naval Court-Martial*, 160.

56. Mackenzie's letter to Secretary Upshur, in *Proceedings of the Naval Court-Martial*, 207.

Chapter 6

1. Brooklyn *Daily Eagle*, December 15, 1842.

2. Brooklyn *Daily Eagle*, December 15, 1842.

3. Mackenzie's letters to Abel Upshur, December 5 and December 14, 1842, in the National Archives, Letters to the Secretary of the Navy; they are cited and quoted from in McFarland, *Sea Dangers*, 153.

4. *Baltimore Sun*, December 19, 1842.

5. New York *Evening Post*, December 22, 1842.

6. Hayford, *The Somers Mutiny Affair*, 1.

7. Rumors and patterns of the coverage are found in the Brooklyn *Evening Star*, December 19, 1842; New York *Daily Tribune*, December 21, 1842; Detroit *Free Press*, December 28, 1842; and New York *Evening Post*, December 21, 1842.

8. New York *Herald*, December 19, 1842.

9. Secretary Spencer's letter appears in the December 20, 1842, edition of the Washington, DC, *Daily Madisonian*.

10. Tuckerman, *The Diary of Philip Hone*, vol. II, 165–166.

11. Letter from Sedgwick to Charles Sumner, dated July 6, 1843, in Sumner's papers at the Houghton Library and quoted in McFarland, *Sea Dangers*, 181, 281.

12. Tuckerman, *The Diary of Philip Hone*, vol. II, 166–167.

13. Letter dated January 11, 1843, and reproduced in the New York *Evening Post*, January 13, 1843.

14. Gregory's report, dated January 7, 1843, is in the National Archives' RG24; McFarland, *Sea Dangers*, 178–179, 280.

15. New York *Tribune*, January 12, 1843. The paper published the entirety of Judge Betts' decision, including his citations of case law.

16. New York *Tribune*, February 2, 1843.

17. New York *Tribune*, January 22, 1843.

18. New York *Tribune*, January 26, 1843.

19. New York *Tribune*, February 2, 1843.

20. Egan, "Secret Correspondence," 151.

21. Tuckerman, *Diary of Philip Hone*, 174–175.

22. The views and noting Griffith's hyperbolic closing statement is from Tuckerman, *Diary of Philip Hone*, 180–181.

23. New York *Tribune*, April 15, 1843, 2.

24. Tuckerman, *Diary of Philip Hone*, 181.

25. New York *Tribune*, February 10, 1843.

26. New York *Tribune*, February 23, 1843, and March 6, 1843.

27. Letter from Watson to Dana, dated February 22, 1843, in the Dana Papers in the collections of the Massachusetts Historical Society, and quoted in Hayford, *The Somers Affair*, 129.

28. The votes against Mackenzie are included in a verbatim transcript of the trial in *Niles National Register*, July 1, 1843.

29. The case of *Wilson v. Mackenzie* was discussed in the Buffalo, New York, *Daily National Pilot*, March 25, 1845, and in the Brooklyn *Evening Star*, April 18, 1846. The State Supreme Court ruling is in Hill, *Reports of Cases*, 95–100.

30. Egan, "The Mackenzie Court-Martial Trial," 150–152.

31. Sumner, "The Mutiny on the Somers," 229.

Chapter 7

1. The account of Leecock's suicide and his death is from "Suicide on the *Somers*," in the Raleigh, North Carolina, *Weekly Standard* of April 12, 1843, republishing an account from the New York *Commercial Advertiser*.

2. The Tarboro, North Carolina, *Tarboro Press*, April 15, 1843.

3. Mecholsky, "Adaptation as Anarchist," 76. I was powerfully drawn to Mecholsky's dissertation, and found resonance in his first words in the abstract: "Bruce Springsteen is considered one of the most quintessential American singer songwriters, and in fact he has said that through his music he tries primarily to judge the distance between American reality and the American Dream. This is a concern with which I feel much sympathy, and in my own professional life I have tried to do something similar: determine what it means to have an American identity in a theoretical sense and in its realistic

sense, define the discrepancy between the two, and articulate a way to bridge that gap by critiquing the stories we tell ourselves," 2.

4. Guttridge, *Mutiny*, 116.

5. Tuckerman, *The Diary of Philip Hone*, 167.

6. Tuckerman, *The Diary of Philip Hone*, 183.

7. Hayford, *The Somers Mutiny Affair*, 159.

8. Letter from John Tyler to Daniel Webster dated November 6, 1851, and reproduced in "Letters of John Tyler," 174, 175, fn.

9. Letter written by Dr. Francis Lieber to his wife from Mackenzie's farm on August 3, 1843, reproduced in Hayford, *The Somers Mutiny Affair*, 179.

10. Parker, *Recollections of a Naval Officer*, 17.

11. Phelps, "Reminiscences of the Old Navy," 815.

12. The Bangor *Daily Whig and Courier*, February 25, 1842.

13. Ambrose Spencer and the Snively expedition are discussed in the Bangor *Daily Whig and Courier*, August 10, 1843.

14. An excellent summary of the life of Ambrose Spencer is found in Davis, "Yankee Gone South: The Georgia Odyssey of 'Colonel Spencer of Andersonville,'" 50–65.

15. "Scraps of History," Jefferson City *State Journal*, April 28, 1876.

16. The accident on USS *Princeton* and the background to the event are excellently summarized by Hagan, *This People's Navy*, 122–123.

17. New York *Tribune*, March 21, 1845.

18. Hayford, *The Somers Mutiny Affair*, 203.

19. Dr. Francis Lieber to his wife from Mackenzie's farm on August 3, 1843, reproduced in Hayford, *The Somers Mutiny Affair*, 178.

20. Dana, as quoted in Hayford, *The Somers Mutiny Affair*, 183.

21. Hayford, *The Somers Mutiny Affair*, 156.

22. The Vermont *Christian Messenger*, September 27, 1848.

23. The poem, by "Horser Clensing, Esq, Quarter Master U. States Service," appeared in the New York *Herald* of May 11, 1843; it is reproduced in Hayford, *The Somers Mutiny Affair*, 164–168.

24. Rogers, "Some Reminiscences of Philip Spencer," 29.

25. Rogers, "Some Reminiscences of Philip Spencer," 31.

26. Rogers, "Some Reminiscences of Philip Spencer," 31–32.

27. Rogers, "Some Reminiscences of Philip Spencer," 35.

28. Rogers, "Some Reminiscences of Philip Spencer," 35–36.

29. St. Louis *Courier Journal*, May 9, 1855.

30. *Louisville Daily Journal*, March 1, 1844.

31. New Orleans *Times Picayune*, September 22, 1844.

32. Snyder's arrest and the circumstances of the assault and murder were summarized in the *Glasgow Herald* of October 17, 1845. The observations on who should have been hanged were noted in the *Southport Telegraph*, October 21, 1845.

33. Buffalo, New York, *Daily National Pilot*, November 27, 1845.

34. Rogers, "Some Reminiscences of Philip Spencer," 28.

35. Semmes, *Memoirs of Service Afloat and Ashore*, 90.

36. Semmes, *Memoirs of Service Afloat and Ashore*, 96.

37. Semmes, *Memoirs of Service Afloat and Ashore*, 96.

Chapter 8

1. Hayford, *The Somers Mutiny Affair*, 197.

2. New York *Weekly Tribune*, December 18, 1842.

3. Letter from Dana, January 11, 1843, cited in Adams, *Dana*, 53.

4. Melville, *White-Jacket*, 284.

5. Brooklyn *Daily Eagle*, November 14, 1886.

6. "Ghastly Tale of the Sea," New Haven *Evening Journal Courier*, April 20, 1898.

7. Washington *Evening Star*, August 9, 1906.

8. "Death Examples: U.S. Army and Navy Summary Executions for Good of the Service" appeared, for example, in the Foraker, Oklahoma, *Tribunal*, January 21, 1910.

9. Andre Sennwald's review of *Mutiny on the Bounty* appeared in the *New York Times*, November 19, 1935.

10. Van de Water, *The Captain Called It Mutiny*, ix.

11. Van de Water, *The Captain Called It Mutiny*, 213 and 13.

12. Morison, *Old Bruin*, 148, 162.

13. Carlisle, *Voyage to the First of December*, 246.

Epilogue

1. Carlisle, *Voyage to the First of December*, 3.

2. Belcher, "Bound for the Devil," 252.

3. The article by Pilar Luna Erreguerena ("Nacimiento y desarrollo de la arqueología subacuática en México") in 2010 and the most recent work by Jorge Herrera and his colleagues ("La memoria anfibia: arqueología marítima de la guerra entre México y los Estados Unidos, 1846–1848") document the exceptional work done by the Mexicans on the wreck.

BIBLIOGRAPHY

MANUSCRIPTS

Belcher, George. "Search for the Ghost Ship *Somers*: An Infamous Brig-of-War Sunk in a Mexican Sea." 2014. Bound photocopied volume, author's collection.

Delgado, James P. U.S. Brig *Somers*, Preliminary Report, 1992. Documentation of the U.S. Brig *Somers* (1842–1846), Veracruz, Mexico, in cooperation with the Government of Mexico, National Park Service Submerged Resources Center, Denver.

Records of the Bureau of Naval Personnel, National Archives Records Group 24, National Archives, Washington, DC, and College Park, Maryland

    24.2   General Records of the Bureau of Naval Personnel and Its Predecessors, 1801–1906

    24.2.1 Correspondence, Office of the Secretary of the Navy

    24.3.1 Records Relating to Naval Officers, 1798–1943

           Registers of Letters Sent, 1823–1884

           Letters Sent to Naval Officers, 1798–1886

           Miscellaneous Letters Sent, 1798–1886

           Miscellaneous Letters Received, 1801–1884

           Letters Sent to Commandants of Navy Yards and Naval Stations and to Navy Agents, 1808–1865

           Officers Letters, 1802–1884

           Letters Received from Commanders, 1804–1886

           Letters Received from Captains, 1805–1861

           Directives, 1798–1911

Muster Rolls, Payrolls, Officer Rolls and Related Records, 1798–1889

Muster Rolls and Payrolls for U.S. Navy Vessels, 1798–1860

Letters of Resignation Received from Commissioned and Warrant Officers

Register of Applications for Appointment as Midshipmen

Letters Received Accepting Appointments as Midshipmen

Register of Midshipmen

Returns of Boys Entered as Apprentices

24.3.2 Records Relating to Enlisted Men, 1798–1943

24.3.3 Records Relating to Naval Apprentices, 1798–1943

Records of the Office of the Judge Advocate General, Navy and Its Predecessors, National Archives Records Group 125, National Archives, Washington, DC, and College Park, Maryland

125.2.2 Personnel Records, Transcripts of Proceedings of General Courts-Martial and Courts of Inquiry, 1799–1867

PUBLISHED SOURCES

Adams, Charles Francis. *Richard Henry Dana, A Biography*. Vol. 1. Boston and New York: Houghton, Mifflin and Company, 1890.

Baldwin, Hanson W. *Admiral Death, Twelve Adventures of Men against the Sea*. New York: Simon & Schuster, 1939.

Barrett, Walter. *The Old Merchants of New York City*. Vol. II. New York: James R. Knox & Co., 1885.

Barton, John Cyril. *Literary Executions: Capital Punishment and American Culture, 1820–1925*. Baltimore: Johns Hopkins University Press, 2014.

Bauer, K. Jack. *Surfboats and Horse Marines: U.S. Naval Operations in the Mexican War, 1846–1848*. Annapolis, MD: Naval Institute Press, 1969.

Beach, Edward L. *The United States Navy: 200 Years*. New York: Henry Holt, 1986.

Belcher, George. "The U.S. Brig *Somers*—a Shipwreck from the Mexican War." In *Underwater Archaeology Proceedings from the Society for Historical Archaeology Conference, Reno, Nevada*. Ann Arbor, MI: Society for Historical Archaeology, 1988.

Beneman, William. *Unruly Desires: American Sailors and Homosexuality's in the Age of Sail*. Independently published, 2019.

Benton, Thomas Hart. *Thirty Years' View; A History of the Working of the American Government for Thirty Years, from 1820 to 1850*. Vol. 2. New York: D. Appleton and Company, 1858.

Biddlecomb, George. *The Art of Rigging: Containing an Alphabetical Explanation of Terms and Phrases . . . and the Progressive Method of Rigging.* London: Charles Wilson, 1848.

Brooke, Henry R. *Highwaymen and Pirates' Own Book: Containing Historical Narratives of the Most Celebrated Robbers, Pirates, &c. Together with an Account of the Loss of the Ship William Brown: and a Full Description of the Mutiny on Board the United States' Brig Somers, with the Execution of Spencer, Cromwell and Small.* New York: John B. Perry, 1847.

Burg, B. R. *The Erotic Diaries of Philip C. Van Buskirk: An American Seafarer in the Age of Sail.* New Haven, CT, and London: Yale University Press, 1994.

Callahan, Edward W. *List of Officers of the Navy of the United States and of the Marine Corps from 1775–1900.* New York: L. R. Hamersly, 1901.

Carlisle, Henry. *Voyage to the First of December.* New York: G. P. Putnam's Sons, 1972.

Carwardine, Richard. *Evangelicals and Politics in Antebellum America.* New Haven, CT, and London: Yale University Press, 1993.

Case of the Somers Mutiny. Defence of Alexander Slidell Mackenzie, Commander of the U.S. Brig Somers, before the Court-Martial held at the Navy Yard, Brookline. New York: Tribune Office, 1843.

Chang, Melinda Y., Federico G. Velez, Joseph L. Demer, Sherwin J. Isenberg, Anne L. Coleman, and Stacy L. Pineles. "Quality of Life in Adults with Strabismus." *American Journal of Ophthalmology* 159, no. 3 (March 2015): 539–544.

Chapelle, Howard I. *The History of the American Sailing Navy: The Ships and Their Development.* New York: W. W. Norton, 1949.

Child, Hamilton. *Gazetteer and Business Directory of Ontario County, New York for 1867–8.* New York: The Syracuse Journal, 1867.

Cooper, James Fenimore. *The Cruise of the Somers: Illustrative of the Despotism of the Quarter Deck and the Unmanly Conduct of Commander Mackenzie.* New York: J. Winchester, 1844.

Culham, Phyllis. "'Strange Characters': The Results of a Classical Education?" *The Classical Outlook* 61, no. 2 (1983): 37–41.

Dana, Richard Henry, Jr. *Two Years before the Mast, and Twenty-Four Years After: A Personal Narrative.* London: Sampson Low, Son & Marston, 1869.

Davis, Robert Scott. "Yankee Gone South: The Georgia Odyssey of 'Colonel Spencer of Andersonville.'" *Georgia Historical Quarterly* 88, no. 1 (Spring 2004): 50–65.

Delgado, James P. *War at Sea: A Shipwrecked History.* New York: Oxford University Press, 2019.

Delgado, James P. "Wreck Site of the U.S. Brig *Somers*." In *Excavating of Ships of War*, ed. Mensun Bound, 276–286. International Maritime Archaeology Series. Ostwestry, Shropshire: Anthony Nelson, 1998.

Delgado, James P., ed. *Underwater Archaeology Proceedings from the Society for Historical Archaeology Conference, Reno, Nevada, 1988.* Ann Arbor, Society for Historical Archaeology, 1989, pp. 91–94.

Dickens, Charles. "Over the Ways Story." *Household Words* 23 (1854), 18–34.

Duban, James, *Melville's Major Fiction: Politics, Theology and Imagination.* Denton: Aquiline Books/University of North Texas Libraries, 1983.

Edwards, Martha L. "Religious Forces in the United States, 1815–1830." *Mississippi Valley Historical Review* 5, no. 4 (March 1919): 434–449.

Egan, Hugh. "The Mackenzie Court-Martial Trial: Cooper's Secret Correspondence with William H. Norris." *Studies in the American Renaissance* (1990): 149–158.

Egan, Pierce. *Every Gentleman's Manual: A Lecture on the Art of Self-Defence.* London: Flinthoff, 1851.

Ellms, Charles. *The Pirates Own Book; or, Authentic Narratives of the Lives, Exploits, and Executions of the Most Celebrated Sea Robbers.* Philadelphia: Thomas, Cowperthwaite & Co., 1837.

Farr, Gail E., and Brett F. Bostwick. *John Lenthall, Naval Architect: A Guide to Plans and Drawings of American Naval and Merchant Vessels, 1790–1874.* Philadelphia: Philadelphia Maritime Museum, 1991.

Ferguson, Robert A. "The *Somers* Mutiny and the American Ship of State." In *The Routledge Research Companion to Law and Humanities in Nineteenth-Century America*, ed. Nan Goodman and Simon Stern, 188–206. London and New York: Routledge, 2017.

Fessenden, Laura Dayton. *Genealogical Story (Dayton and Tomlinson).* Cooperstown, NY: Crist, Scott & Parshall, 1902.

Feuer, A. B. "A Question of Mutiny." *Naval History* 8, no. 2 (March–April 1994): 22–27.

Franklin, Wayne. *James Fenimore Cooper: The Later Years.* New Haven, CT, and London: Yale University Press, 2017.

Friedman, Lawrence J., and David Curtis Skaggs. "Jesse Duncan Elliott and the Battle of Lake Erie: The Issue of Mental Stability." *Journal of the Early Republic* 10, no. 4 (1990): 493–516.

"Froissart and His Chronicle, No. VI." *Knight's Penny Magazine* 40, no. 2 (September 10, 1842): 353.

Fuller, Edmund, ed. *Mutiny: Being Accounts of Insurrections, Famous and Infamous, on Land and Sea, from the Days of the Caesars to Modern Times.* New York: Crown, 1953.

Garcia-Bárcena, Joaquin. "El brig U.S.S. *Somers.*" *Arqueología Mexicana* 18, no. 105 (2010): 39–42.

Gay, William W. "Some Recollections of Spencer." *The Purple and Gold* 2, no. 2 (April 1885): 37.

Glenn, Myra C. *Jack Tar's Story: The Autobiographies and Memoirs of Sailors in Antebellum America.* Cambridge: Cambridge University Press, 2010.

"A Glimpse at Our Navy." *The Advocate of Peace* 3, no. 8 (August 1840): 187–190.

Goldberg, Angus Ephraim. "The *Somers* Mutiny of 1842." PhD diss., University of St. Andrews, August 1999. http://hdl.handle.net/10023/2695.

Gouverneur, Marian Campbell. *As I Remember: Recollection of American Society during the Nineteenth Century.* New York: D. Appleton and Company, 1911.

Griffis, William Elliot. *Matthew Calbraith Perry: A Typical American Naval Officer.* Boston: Cupples and Hurd, 1887.

Guttridge, Leonard F. *A History of Naval Insurrection.* Annapolis, MD: Naval Institute Press, 1992.

Hagan, Kenneth J. *This People's Navy: The Making of American Sea Power.* New York: Simon & Schuster, 1992.

Hall, Claude H. *Abel Parker Upshur: Conservative Virginian, 1790–1844.* Madison: State Historical Society of Wisconsin, 1964.

Halperin, David M. *One Hundred Years of Homosexuality and Other Essays in Greek Love.* New York: Routledge, 1990.

Hamilton, Gail. "The Murder of Philip Spencer." *Cosmopolitan Magazine* 7 (June, July, August 1889): 133–140, 248–256, and 345–354.

Hayford, Harrison, ed. *The Somers Mutiny Affair.* Englewood Cliffs, NJ: Prentice-Hall, 1959.

Herrera, Jorge M., Pamela Jiménez, Rodrigo Pacheco Ruiz, Jorge Blancas, Agustín Ortiz Butrón, Luis Barba, Rodrigo Vega Sánchez, Martha Arenas Cruz, Diana Mata, Eduardo Castillo Pérez, Daniel A. Ortiz Nieto, Erick Sealtiel Rodríguez, and Guadalupe Martínez. "La memoria anfibia: arqueología marítima de la guerra entre México y los Estados Unidos, 1846–1848." In *Arqueología en campos de batalla: América Latina en perspectiva*, ed. Landa and Hernández-de-Lara, 31–84. Buenos Aires: ASPHA, 2020.

Hill, Nicholas, ed. *Reports of Cases Argued and Determined in the Supreme Court and in the Court for the Correction of Errors of the State of New York.* New York: Banks & Brothers, 1883.

Historical Society of the New York Courts. "Wilson v. Mackenzie, 1845." 7 Hill 95 (1845). https://history.nycourts.gov/case/wilson-v-mackenzie/.

Horner, Gustavus R. B. *The Diseases and Injuries of Seamen, with Remarks on Their Enlistment, Naval Hygiene, and the Duties of Medical Officers.* Philadelphia: Lippincott and Grambo, 1854.

Howe, Daniel Walker. *What Hath God Wrought: The Transformation of America, 1815–1848.* New York: Oxford University Press, 2007.

Howe, David. "Essay on the Legal Aspects of *Somers* Affair and Bibliography." https://www.history.navy.mil/research/library/online-reading-room/title-list-alphabetically/s/somers-essay-on-legal-aspects-of-somers-aff air.html.

Howe, Samuel Storrs. "My Schools and Scholars. No. IV." *Annals of Iowa* 1 (1884): 23–31. http://digitalcommons.conncoll.edu/histhp/1.

Hunt, Admiral Livingston. "The Attempted Mutiny on the U.S. Brig 'Somers.'" *United States Naval Institute Proceedings* 51, no. 273 (November 1925): 2062–2100.

Inquiry into the Somers Mutiny: With a Full Account of the Execution of Spencer, Cromwell and Small. New York: Greeley & McElrath, 1843.

Irving, Pierre M. *The Life and Letters of Washington Irving.* Vol. 2. New York: G. P. Putnam's Sons, 1862.

Karp, Matthew J. "Slavery and American Sea Power: The Navalist Impulse in the Antebellum South." *Journal of Southern History* 77, no. 2 (2011): 283–324.

Ketterer, David. "Some Co-Ordinates in 'Billy Budd.'" *Journal of American Studies* 3, no. 2 (1969): 221–237.

Landa, Carlos G., and Odlanyer Hernández-de-Lara, eds. *Arqueología en campos de batalla: América Latina en perspectiva.* Buenos Aires: ASPHA, 2020.

Langley, Harold D. *Social Reform in the United States Navy, 1789–1862.* Annapolis, MD: Naval Institute Press, 1967, 2015.

Lee, Jennie. *My Life with Nye.* London: Cape Books, 1980.

Leeman, John P. *The Long Road to Annapolis: The Founding of the Naval Academy and the Emerging American Republic.* Chapel Hill: University of North Carolina Press, 2010.

Lehman, John F. *On Seas of Glory: Heroic Men, Great Ships, and Epic Battles of the American Navy.* New York: Free Press, 2001.

"Letters of John Tyler." *William and Mary Quarterly* 18, no. 3 (1910): 172–176.

Lever, Darcy. *The Young Sea Officer's Sheet Anchor; or, A Key to the Leading of Rigging and to Practical Seamanship.* London: John Richardson, 1819.

Liebling, A. J. "The Navy's Only Mutiny." *New Yorker,* February 18, 1939, 35.

Longworth, D., comp. *American Almanac New-York Register and City-Directory, for the Twenty-Eighth Year of American Independence.* New York: D. Longworth, 1804.

Lounsbury, Thomas R. *American Men of Letters; James Fenimore Cooper.* Boston: Houghton, Mifflin and Company, 1884.

Luna Erreguerena, Pilar. "Nacimiento y desarrollo de la arqueología sub-acuática en México." *Arqueología Mexicana* 18, no. 105 (2010): 24–28.

Luna Erreguerena, Pilar, and James P. Delgado. "The U.S. Naval Brig *Somers*: A Mexican War Shipwreck of 1846." Paper Presented at the Society for Historical Archaeology, Washington, DC, 2016.

Mackenzie, Alexander Slidell. *Life of Stephen Decatur, a Commodore in the Navy of the United States.* Boston: Charles C. Little and James Brown, 1846.

Marovitz, Sanford E. "Melville among the Realists: W. D. Howells and the Writing of 'Billy Budd.'" *American Literary Realism* 34, no. 1 (Fall 2001): 29–46.

McBain, H. B., K. A. MacKenzie, C. Au, J. Hancox, D. G. Ezra, G. G. W. Adams, and S. P. Newman. "Factors Associated with Quality of Life and Mood in Adults with Strabismus." *British Journal of Ophthalmology* 98, no. 4 (2014): 550–555.

McFarland, Philip. *Sea Dangers: The Affair of the Somers.* New York: Schocken Books, 1985.

McKee, Christopher. "Fantasies of Mutiny and Murder: A Suggested Psycho-History of the Seaman in the United States Navy, 1798–1815." *Armed Forces & Society* 4, no. 2 (Winter 1978): 293–304.

McKee, Christopher, *A Gentlemanly and Honorable Profession: The Creation of the U.S. Naval Officer Corps, 1794–1815.* Annapolis, MD: Naval Institute Press, 1991.

McNally, William. *Evils and Abuses in the Naval and Merchant Service, Exposed: With Proposals for Their Remedy and Redress.* Boston: Cassady and March, 1839.

Mecholsky, Kristopher. "Adaptation as Anarchist: A Complexity Method for Ideology-Critique of American Crime Narratives." LSU Doctoral Dissertations 3247 (2012). https://digitalcommons.lsu.edu/gradschool_dissertations/3247.

Melton, Buckner F. *A Hanging Offense: The Strange Affair of the Warship Somers.* New York: Free Press, 2003.

Melville, Herman. *Billy Budd: Sailor (An Inside Narrative).* Edited and annotated by Harrison Hayford and Merton M. Sealts Jr. Chicago and London: University of Chicago Press, 1962.

Melville, Herman. *Poems Containing Battle-Pieces, John Marr and Other Sailors, Timoleon and Miscellaneous Poems*. London: Constable and Company, 1924.

Melville, Herman. *White Jacket; or, The World in a Man-of-War*. Boston: St. Botolph Society, 1892.

Miller, Kerby A. *Emigrants and Exiles: Ireland and the Irish Exodus to North America*. New York: Oxford University Press, 1985.

Milliken, Charles F. *A History of Ontario County, New York and Its People*. Vol. 1. New York: Lewis Historical Publishing Company, 1911.

Mills, Eric. *The Spectral Tide: True Ghost Stories of the U.S. Navy*. Annapolis, MD: Naval Institute Press, 2013.

Mintz, Steven. *Moralists and Modernizers: America's Pre–Civil War Reformers*. Baltimore: Johns Hopkins University Press, 1995.

Morison, Samuel Eliot. *"Old Bruin": Commodore Matthew Perry, 1794–1858*. Boston: Little, Brown, 1967.

Morris, H. H. "The USS *Somers* Affair." *American History Illustrated* 9, no. 5 (August 1974): 24–30.

Naval History and Heritage Command. U.S. Navy Brig *Somers*. https://www.history.navy.mil/browse-by-topic/ships/ships-of-sail/us-navy-brig-somers.html.

Nelson, Bradley, Kammi Gunton, Judith Lasker, Leonard Nelson, and Lea Drohan. "The Psychosocial Aspects of Strabismus in Teenagers and Adults and the Impact of Surgical Correction." *Journal of AAPOS* 12 (2008): 72–76.

Nordhoff, Charles. *Man-of-War Life*. New York: Dodd, Mead & Company, 1895.

Nugent, Walter. "The American Habit of Empire, and the Cases of Polk and Bush." *Western Historical Quarterly* 38, no. 1 (2007): 4–24.

Oakes, James, et al. *Of the People: A History of the United States*. Vol. 1, *To 1877*. New York: Oxford University Press, 2010.

Parker, William H. *Recollections of a Naval Officer, 1841–1865*. New York: Scribner's, 1883.

Parmelee, T. N. "Recollections of an Old Stager: The *Somers* Tragedy." *Harpers Monthly* 46, no. 275 (April 1873): 700–704.

Paullin, Charles Oscar. *Commodore John Rodgers, Captain, Commodore, and Senior Officer of the American Navy, 1773–1838: A Biography*. Cleveland: Arthur H. Clark Co., 1910.

Paullin, Charles Oscar. "Dueling in the Old Navy." *United States Naval Institute Proceedings* 35, no. 132 (1909): 1155–1197.

Paullin, Charles Oscar. "Naval Administration 1842–1861." *United States Naval Institute Proceedings* 33, no. 124 (1907): 1435–1477.

Paullin, Charles Oscar. "Naval Administration under the Navy Commissioners, 1815–1842." *United States Naval Institute Proceedings* 33, no. 117 (1907): 597–641.

Pearson, Lee M. "The 'Princeton' and the 'Peacemaker': A Study in Nineteenth-Century Naval Research and Development Procedures." *Technology and Culture* 7, no. 2 (Spring 1966): 163–183.

Pearson, Norman Holmes. "Billy Budd: 'The King's Yarn.'" *American Quarterly* 3, no. 2 (1951): 99–114.

Phelps, Thomas. "The Moral Character of the Navy." *The Advocate of Peace* 3, no. 8 (August 1840): 184–187.

Phelps, Thomas. "Reminiscences of the Old Navy." *The United Service* 3, no. 2 (February 1903): 815.

Post, Alfred C. *Observations on the Cure of Strabismus, with Engravings.* New York: Charles S. Francis, 1841.

Powers, Rod. "Navy Fraternization Policies, OPNAV Instruction 5370.2B." https://www.thebalancecareers.com/navy-fraternization-policies-3354650, revised July 15, 2019, reviewed June 24, 2021.

Proceedings of the Court of Inquiry Appointed to Inquire into the Intended Mutiny on Board the United States Brig of War Somers, on the High Seas; Held on Board the United States Ship North Carolina Lying at the Navy Yard, New York; With a Full Account of the Execution of Spencer, Cromwell and Small, on Board Said Vessel, Reported for the New York Tribune. New York: Greeley & McElrath, 1843.

Proceedings of the Naval Court-Martial in the Case of Alexander Slidell Mackenzie, a Commander in the Navy of the United States, &c., Including the Charges and Specifications of Charges Preferred against Him by the Secretary of the Navy. To Which is Annexed an Elaborate Review by James Fenimore Cooper. New York: Henry G. Langley, 1844.

Ray, George W., ed. *The Chi Psi Story.* Ann Arbor, MI: Chi Psi Educational Trust, 1995.

Richardson, James D., ed. *A Compilation of the Messages and Papers of the Presidents, 1789–1908.* Vol. III. Washington, DC: Bureau of National Literature and Art, 1897.

Rockwell, C. *Sketches of Foreign Travel and Life at Sea; Including a Cruise on Board a Man-of-War.* Vol. 1. Boston: Tappan and Dennet, 1842.

Rogers, Robert C. "Some Reminiscences of Philip Spencer and the Brig 'Somers.'" *The United Service* 4 (July 1890): 23–36.

Rorabaugh, W. J. *The Alcoholic Republic: An American Tradition.* New York: Oxford University Press, 1979.

Rutz, Paul X. "The *Somers* Mutiny: Justice from the Yardarms, Historynet, March 2021." https://www.historynet.com/the-somers-mutiny-justice-from-the-yardarms.htm.

Seger, Slifer H., and Hiram L. Kennicott, eds. *The Chi Psi Story.* Ann Arbor, MI: Chi Psi, 1951.

Semmes, Raphael. *Service Afloat and Ashore during the Mexican War.* Cincinnati: William H. More, 1851.

Seward, Frederick W. *William H. Seward: An Autobiography, from 1801 to 1834, with a Memoir of His Life, and Selections from His Letters, 1831–1846.* New York: Derby and Miller, 1891.

Sioussat, George L. "The Accident on Board the U.S.S. 'Princeton,' February 28, 1844: A Contemporary News-Letter." *Pennsylvania History: A Journal of Mid-Atlantic Studies* 4, no. 3 (1937): 161–189.

Smith, H. D. "The Mutiny of the *Somers.*" *American Magazine* 8 (June 1888): 109–114.

Southworth, Eve. "Drunken Sailors and Fallen Women." History Honors Papers, Connecticut College 1. 2005.

Spencer, John C. *American Institutions and Their Influence by Alexis de Tocqueville.* New York: A. S. Barnes & Company, 1851.

Sumner, Charles. "The Mutiny of the Somers." *North American Review* 67 (July 1843): 195–241.

"Ticknor's Spanish Literature." *Methodist Review* 10 (April 1850): 295.

"Trade of Porto Rico." *Simmonds's Colonial Magazine and Foreign Miscellany* 2, no. 5 (May 1844): 103–104.

Tuckerman, Bayard, ed. *The Diary of Philip Hone, 1828–1851.* 2 vols. New York: Dodd, Mead and Company, 1889.

Twain, Mark. *The Jumping Frog, in English, Then in French, Then Clawed Back into a Civilized Language Once More by Patient, Unremunerated Toil.* New York and London: Harper and Brothers, Publishers, 1903.

U.S. Naval Academy. "The Somers Affair." USNA Digital Collections. https://cdm16099.contentdm.oclc.org/digital/collection/p15241coll1.

Valle, James E. *Rocks and Shoals: Naval Discipline in the Age of Fighting Sail.* Annapolis, MD: Naval Institute Press/Blue Jacket Books, 1980.

Van de Water, Frederic F. *The Captain Called It Mutiny.* New York: Ives Washburn, Inc., 1954.

Van de Water, Frederic F. "Panic Rides the High Seas." *American Heritage* 12, no. 4 (June 1961): 20–23, 97–99.

Vaughan, William Preston. *The Antimasonic Party in the United States, 1826–1843*. Lexington: University Press of Kentucky, 1983.

Vazquez de la Cerda, Alberto. "El hundamiento del *Somers*." *Revista Secretaría de Marina* 4, no. 67 (March–April 1993): 32–36.

Vickers, Daniel, and Vince Walsh. *Young Men and the Sea: Yankee Seafarers in the Age of Sail*. New Haven, CT, and London: Yale University Press, 2005.

Walters, Ronald G. *American Reformers, 1815–1860*. Rev. ed. New York: Hill & Wang, 1997.

Webster, Daniel. *The Writings and Speeches of Daniel Webster: Writings and Speeches Hitherto Uncollected, Letters*. Vol. 4, National Edition, Vol. 16. Boston: Little, Brown and Company, 1903.

Weed, Harriet, ed. *Autobiography of Thurlow Weed*. Boston: Houghton, Mifflin and Company, 1884.

White, James Terry, ed. *National Encyclopaedia of American Biography*. Vol. 6. New York: James T. White & Co., 1892–1930.

INDEX